desserts IN *jars*

50 **SWEET TREATS THAT SHINE**

SHAINA OLMANSON

THE HARVARD COMMON PRESS
BOSTON, MASSACHUSETTS

The Harvard Common Press
535 Albany Street
Boston, Massachusetts 02118
www.harvardcommonpress.com

Printed in China
Printed on acid-free paper

Library of Congress Cataloging-in-Publication Data
Olmanson, Shaina.
    Desserts in jars : 50 sweet treats that shine / Shaina Olmanson.
      p. cm.
    Includes index.
    ISBN 978-1-55832-798-6 (spiral bound)
1. Desserts. 2. Storage jars. 3. Cookware. I. Title.
    TX773.O46 2012
    641.86—dc23
                                        2012000320

Special bulk-order discounts are available on this and other Harvard
Common Press books. Companies and organizations may purchase
books for premiums or resale, or may arrange a custom edition, by
contacting the Marketing Director at the address above.

Author photograph by Stephanie Meyer

10 9 8 7 6 5 4 3 2

For my grandmother, who taught me how to give a piece of myself through the food I make.

contents

introduction
a dessert in a jar

They are a trend today, but desserts in jars in fact are timeless. A number of friends have shared with me that their grandmothers tucked desserts into their canning jars, for backyard garden parties or Sunday afternoon picnics. The jars were what they had at hand, and really, the practicality of it makes sense.

In a day and age where so much of what we use day in and day out is disposable, using glass jars as a serving mechanism or a gifting vessel for dessert is a way to make the entire package reusable. Whether you go on to put up food in them after the dessert is long gone or repurpose them for another household use, jars are containers that have a multitude of usage possibilities.

Eco-friendly and multi-purposeful, glass jars win points for aesthetics as well. They can be a cute and decorative gift that requires just a simple ribbon and gift tag as packaging, and they can also find a place at a respectable dinner party. They can be well received and at home during an outdoor vintage wedding.

They are easy to package and carry with just a lid, a towel, and a sturdy basket or box. Desserts in jars require no plate or bowl, making them less susceptible to landing in your lap or on the ground next to you while eating outdoors. All that is necessary is a proper utensil, a simple fork or spoon, and you'll be on your way to digging into a delicious treat.

CHOOSING THE PERFECT JARS

There are a variety of canning and Mason jars on the market, in many different sizes, prices, and designs, and with a range of closing mechanisms. This leaves a world of possibilities out there to explore when you're looking at serving dessert to guests, shipping jars in the mail, or giving mixes as gifts. You always want to use clean, chip-free jars. Never use jars that have been chipped or cracked in any way. Two more things to consider are the size of the opening or mouth of the jar and the height of the jar from the mouth to the bottom.

First, let's consider the jar opening or "mouth." Jars typically come in one of two sizes of opening: standard or wide-mouth. Most standard jar openings are 2⅜ inches in diameter, while wide-mouth openings are 3⅛ inches across. There are other styles of jars that have openings specific to the brand or design of the jar. When making a dessert that requires you to reach into the jar to pack it, as you will do with a cheesecake crust or a layered parfait, a wide-mouth opening will give you more room with which to work.

Next let's look at the height of the jar. There are several reasons you may choose one height over another, from presentation to ease of eating, but the most important thing to consider is content. When filling a jar with a layered dessert where you ideally want one fork- or spoonful to contain all layers of the dessert, a shorter jar will make the process much easier. Taller jars can be used for desserts without layers, such as the Almond-Poppy Seed Cakes, page 39, or ones with a liquid component, such as the Peach Granita Bellinis, page 127. These types of desserts lend themselves well to jars with taller sides.

Finally, think of the serving size of the dessert that will be presented in the jar. While the recipes in this book suggest an approximate jar size, you'll want to use jars that provide an appropriate serving. Exact jar sizes can differ from company to company, but for single-serve desserts you want to look for jars in the 4- to 8-ounce range. For mixes the jar size will be determined by the recipe but generally are best when packaged in pint- or quart-sized jars. The recipes in this book give guidance for jar sizes that are appropriate to them.

FILLING JARS

Just as when you fill muffin cups, frost cupcakes, make cake pops, or roll out cookie dough, filling jars with doughs, batters, or custards works best when you follow a few tips and use a few tools that help make the process go more smoothly.

Scoops (often called "cookie scoops" or "baking scoops") work great for adding cake batter and puddings to jars. Simply scoop up the appropriate amount of batter or filling and drop it into the jar opening.

Pastry bags and tips are great tools to have on hand when frosting cakes like the Vanilla Bean Cupcakes, page 17, and they also make it easy to pipe puddings or mousse into jars. Zip-top bags are an easy item you may have on hand that can substitute for pastry bags.

While not necessary, funnels can come in handy when adding liquids to jars. You'll want to use funnels that are appropriate for the jar size or the consistency of the liquid. A canning funnel works well when adding heated jams or jellies, and also comes in handy when adding the chocolate cream mixture for the Dark Chocolate Hazelnut *Pots de Crème*, page 77, or when making Sweet Corn Panna Cotta, page 87.

BAKING IN JARS

Some of the recipes in this book require you to bake cakes or custards in the jars. There are two different methods you will see: one uses a baking sheet, the other a water bath. As when baking with any type of glass container, extreme fluctuations in temperature can cause the glass to break. This is similar to when you use jars for canning: You wouldn't want to move hot jars from a hot water bath directly to a cold, flat surface. Likewise, we want to keep hot jars fresh from the oven from coming in contact with cold surfaces and extremely cold jars from being placed in hot ovens.

BAKING DESSERTS IN JARS ON A BAKING SHEET

Many of the cakes, pies, and pastries in this book are baked on a baking sheet. After your oven has preheated and your jars are filled with the batter, place them on a baking sheet 1 to 2 inches apart from each other. Place the baking sheet in the oven and bake as directed. When the desserts are finished baking, remove the sheet from the oven to a clean, dry surface insulated with a dry towel or hot pads and allow to cool.

BAKING JARS IN A WATER BATH

For some recipes like cheesecakes, baked custards, and crèmes, the jars are baked in a water bath. You line a high-sided metal baking pan with a clean kitchen towel, then add the filled jars to the pan 2 to 3 inches apart. Place the baking pan containing the jars in the preheated oven and then carefully pour hot water into the pan using a heat-safe pitcher or tea kettle. When the desserts are finished baking, carefully remove the cake pan from the oven to a clean, dry surface insulated with a dry towel or hot pads and allow to cool.

FREEZING JARS

Whether you're creating delicious desserts from the Frozen Desserts chapter of this book or just looking to freeze already-baked desserts for consumption at a later date, there are a few things you'll want to remember when putting glass jars in the freezer.

When matter freezes, it expands, so leaving headroom or extra space at the top of the jar is important when placing jars in the freezer. This will give the food enough room to expand as it freezes and will prevent breakage from too-full jars. Alternatively, you could always freeze first with the jar covered in plastic wrap until the contents are mostly solid and then add the lids after the contents have expanded.

ADORNMENTS AND GIFT TAGS

Whether you're setting a scene for a backyard party, planning a dessert table for a wedding or shower, or giving food gifts for holidays or as hostess gifts, you may want to decorate and adorn the jars with ribbons, tags, and toppers. Here are a few ideas to get you started.

LID COVERS

Let's start with the most straightforward task: covering the lids. Whether you use a soft paper or cloth, simply trace a circle around the jar lid and make the circle one inch larger the whole way around. Place the cloth or paper on the lid and secure either with the ring closure on the jar or with string, ribbon, or twine.

RIBBONS AND WHATNOT

When tying ribbons or twine around the jars, the easiest way to make sure you have enough string is to do a test jar first without cutting. Then untie the piece of ribbon from the successful test jar and cut lengths of ribbon to match for the remaining jars.

GIFT TAGS AND LABELS

Gift tags or labels are a great way to personalize your desserts and add a bit of character to the jars. They're also necessary for the Mixes chapter, pages 128–145, for giving the recipient directions on how to bake the contents of their jar.

There are plenty of ways to customize tags, from using store-bought tags or pieces you create on your computer (or download from the Internet) to handmade decorations. For the recipes in the chapter on mixes in jars, beginning on page 128, a free set of printable tags, including directions for making the mixes, can be found online at www.dessertsinjars.com.

JARS

The most widely available jars in the United States are going to be Ball and Kerr jars, which are easy to find at supermarkets and hardware stores. I also like to use Weck, Leifheit, and Bormioli Rocco jars, all of which appear in photographs in this book. These brands are available online and in specialty stores. Finally, old and antique jars can be unique and original choices when you can find them in "like new" condition with no chips, cracks, or scratches.

You can find useful information at the websites of these jar manufacturers:

Ball and Kerr jars:
www.freshpreserving.com

Bormioli Rocco jars:
www.bormioliroccousa.com

Leifheit jars:
www.leifheitusa.com

Weck jars:
www.weckjars.com

cakes

and cupcakes

peanut butter cup cupcakes 14

vanilla bean cupcakes with
whipped vanilla buttercream 17

tres leches cakes 20

neapolitan cakes 23

caramel crème cheesecakes 25

orange–white chocolate
cheesecakes with
cranberry sauce 29

pumpkin cheesecakes
with a gingersnap crust 31

flourless chocolate cakes 35

pull-apart cinnamon breads 36

almond–poppy seed cakes 39

peanut butter cup cupcakes

cupcakes

FOR THE CUPCAKES

1½ cups granulated sugar

2 cups all-purpose flour

¾ cup Dutch-process cocoa powder

1 teaspoon baking powder

1½ teaspoons baking soda

½ teaspoon salt

2 large eggs

1 cup vegetable oil

¾ cup buttermilk

1 teaspoon vanilla extract

¾ cup hot coffee or boiling water

FOR THE PEANUT BUTTER FILLING

¾ cup creamy peanut butter

1½ cups confectioners' sugar

FOR THE TOPPING

6 ounces dark chocolate, cut or broken into 12 pieces roughly equal in size

MAKES 12 individual cupcakes

Some things are meant to go together, and peanut butter and

chocolate have long been a combination worth marrying over and over again. Children and adults both will enjoy this dessert; the kids are likely to squeal when they find the creamy peanut butter surprise hidden beneath a layer of chocolate and tucked inside soft devil's food cake.

——————— • ———————

1 Make the cupcakes: Preheat the oven to 350°F. In a large bowl, sift together the granulated sugar, flour, cocoa, baking powder, baking soda, and salt. In a separate bowl, beat together the eggs, oil, buttermilk, and vanilla. Mix the wet ingredients into the dry ingredients. Whisk in the hot coffee just until incorporated. Set aside.

2 Make the filling: In a separate bowl, mix together the peanut butter and confectioners' sugar until smooth. Roll into twelve balls 1½ to 2 inches in diameter. Scoop about 3½ tablespoons of cupcake batter into the bottom of each of twelve 8-ounce jars. Place a peanut butter ball in the center of each jar and cover with an additional 2 to 3 tablespoons of batter. Wipe up any batter from the outside of the jar or around its rim.

3 Place the jars 2 inches apart on a large baking sheet. Bake the cupcakes for 18 to 20 minutes, until the tops spring back when touched. Remove from the oven, immediately place one of the chocolate pieces on top of each hot cupcake, and allow the chocolate to melt. Using hot pads, carefully tilt each jar so that the melted chocolate covers the surface of the cake. Let the cakes cool, and serve at room temperature.

vanilla bean cupcakes

with whipped vanilla buttercream

1½ cups all-purpose flour

1½ cups cake flour

2 teaspoons baking powder

¼ teaspoons salt

1 cup (2 sticks) unsalted butter, softened

2 cups granulated sugar

4 large eggs, separated

1 cup half-and-half

1 teaspoon vanilla extract

Vanilla bean seeds scraped from 1 vanilla bean pod

FOR THE VANILLA BUTTERCREAM

½ cup plus 1 tablespoon heavy cream

3 cups confectioners' sugar

1 cup (2 sticks) unsalted butter, softened

1 teaspoon vanilla extract

There's something magical in the simplicity of a vanilla

cupcake. It's a blank canvas waiting to be painted with buttercream, filled with jams, or drizzled with caramel. This playful take on classic birthday cupcakes allows your guests to participate. Serve these vanilla-on-vanilla cupcakes with a condiment bar to allow your guests to choose their favorite toppings.

———— • ————

1 Preheat the oven to 325°F. Line enough muffin tins with paper liners to make 24 standard-size cupcakes. Make the cupcakes: Sift together the all-purpose flour, cake flour, baking powder, and salt into a bowl and set aside. Cream together the butter and sugar for 2 to 3 minutes until light and fluffy. Add in the egg yolks one at a time, beating after each addition to incorporate. Mix in the half-and-half, vanilla extract, and vanilla bean seeds.

2 In a separate bowl, beat the egg whites until soft peaks form. Fold the egg whites into the batter until incorporated. Fill the liners ⅔ full with the batter. Bake for 20 to 22 minutes, or until the cupcakes are lightly golden on top. Remove from the oven and let cool completely.

recipe continues

Chocolate sauce (recipe, page 123, or store-bought)

Caramel sauce (recipe, page 25, or store-bought)

Raspberry sauce

Sprinkles

MAKES 24 individual cupcakes

3 Make the vanilla buttercream: Beat the ½ cup heavy cream just until stiff peaks form. Set aside. In a stand mixer or using a handheld mixer, cream together the confectioners' sugar and the butter for 2 to 3 minutes until fluffy. Add in the remaining 1 tablespoon of heavy cream and the vanilla. Fold in the whipped cream.

4 Frost the cupcakes by placing the buttercream in a pastry bag and piping onto the cupcakes or by spreading the buttercream with a knife.

5 Have your guests place 1 to 2 tablespoons of their choice of sauce into a 4-ounce jar. Top with an unwrapped frosted cupcake, and serve, with sprinkles on top if you or your guests like.

desserts in jars for a child's birthday party

Children love hands-on activities, and desserts in jars can give them the opportunity to do a variety of them. Consider a dessert that will get them involved, like the Vanilla Bean Cupcakes, page 17. A dessert buffet with sauces, flavored syrups, and fun sprinkles will let kids get involved in putting the finishing touches on their party desserts.

Here are some ideas:

SAUCES OR SYRUPS: strawberry sauce or syrup, raspberry sauce or syrup, chocolate sauce (recipe, page 123), caramel sauce (recipe, page 25)

TOPPINGS: chocolate candies, jimmies, cinnamon sugar, vanilla chips, gummy bears and candies, marshmallows (recipe, page 140)

After dessert, the fun with jars can continue. Large tubs of soapy water can be used to let the kids wash out their own jars. Once dried, the jars can be decorated with ribbons and stickers to create pencil holders, or they could be filled with dirt and used to plant a small flower plant or a seed. The possibilities are endless, and the kids will have fun getting creative with their food and then with their craft.

tres leches
cakes

FOR THE SPONGE CAKE

1½ cups cake flour

¾ teaspoon baking powder

¼ teaspoon salt

6 tablespoons (¾ stick) unsalted butter, softened

½ cup granulated sugar

3 large eggs

1 teaspoon vanilla extract

1 cup sweetened condensed milk

1 cup evaporated milk

½ cup half-and-half

FOR THE TOPPING

1 cup heavy cream

3 tablespoons confectioners' sugar

½ teaspoon vanilla extract

14 maraschino cherries, for garnish

MAKES 14 individual *tres leches* cakes

"Tres leches" is Spanish for "three milks." The cakes that

bear this name are sponge cakes that are literally soaked in those three milks until they have an almost custard-like consistency. Delightful alternatives to frosting-laden birthday cakes, these are topped simply with sweetened whipped cream and a cherry.

———————— • ————————

1 Preheat the oven to 350°F. Line enough muffin tins with paper liners to make 14 cupcake-size cakes. Whisk the cake flour, baking powder, and salt together in a bowl and set aside. Cream the butter for 2 minutes on high speed, then beat in the sugar. Add the eggs one at a time, mixing to incorporate after each addition. Mix in the vanilla. Mix in flour mixture gradually until just combined. Scoop the batter into the cupcake compartments, filling them ⅔ full.

2 Bake the cakes for 18 to 22 minutes, rotating the pans 180 degrees after 9 or 10 minutes, until the tops are lightly browned. Remove from the oven and let cool completely on a cooling rack. Unwrap the cupcakes from their liners. Poke each cake all over with a fork and place each in a 4-ounce jar.

3 Stir together the sweetened condensed milk, evaporated milk, and half-and-half. Spoon 3 to 4 tablespoons of the milk mixture slowly over each cake. Cover the jars and store them in the refrigerator overnight.

4 Before serving, make the topping: Whip together the cream, confectioners' sugar, and vanilla until stiff peaks form. Spread or pipe over the cakes and top with a maraschino cherry.

neapolitan cakes

FOR THE STRAWBERRY CAKE

2½ cups cake flour

1½ cups granulated sugar

2½ teaspoons baking powder

¼ teaspoon salt

12 tablespoons (1½ sticks) unsalted butter, softened

8 ounces fresh strawberries, hulled and pureed, preferably, or ¾ cup frozen strawberry puree

4 large egg whites

½ cup whole milk

FOR THE WHITE AND CHOCOLATE CAKES

2½ cups cake flour

2 teaspoons baking powder

¼ teaspoon salt

1 cup (2 sticks) unsalted butter, softened

2 cups granulated sugar

4 large eggs, at room temperature

½ cup whole milk, at room temperature

For most of us, the word "Neapolitan" evokes memories

of peeling back a thin layer of film from an ice-cream square and revealing the tri-colored frozen cream beneath. Here the strawberry, vanilla, and chocolate come together in cake form, all topped off with a pretty spiral swirl of frosting. This recipe makes a large batch of cupcake-sized desserts. Full of nostalgia and whimsy, it's perfect for a child's birthday party or any kind of backyard bash.

———— • ————

1 Preheat the oven to 350°F. Spray the insides of twenty-four 4-ounce jars with canola oil.

2 Make the strawberry cake batter: Sift together the flour, sugar, baking powder, and salt in a large bowl. Add the butter and strawberry puree, and beat, starting slowly and then more quickly, for 2 to 3 minutes, until you have a very thick batter. In a separate bowl, beat the egg whites until frothy, then whisk in the milk. Add ⅓ cup of the egg white mixture to the batter, then beat until incorporated. Repeat until all the egg white mixture is incorporated. Be sure to scrape down the sides of the bowl as you go. When all the egg white mixture has been added, set the batter aside.

3 Make the white and chocolate cake batters: Sift together the flour, baking powder, and salt in a large bowl and set aside. In another large bowl, cream the butter and sugar until smooth.

recipe continues

½ cup heavy cream, at room temperature

1 teaspoon vanilla extract

¼ cup hot coffee, or ¼ cup boiling water

½ cup unsweetened Dutch-process cocoa powder

FOR THE FROSTING

2 cups (4 sticks) unsalted butter, softened

4 cups confectioners' sugar

2 tablespoons heavy cream, plus more as needed

3 strawberries, hulled and pureed

2 ounces bittersweet chocolate, melted

½ teaspoon vanilla extract

MAKES 24 individual cakes

Beat in the eggs, one at a time. In a separate bowl, combine the milk and cream. Stir ⅓ cup of the milk mixture into the butter mixture, and then stir ⅓ cup of the flour mixture into the butter mixture. Continue alternating additions of milk and flour until they are fully incorporated into the batter. Stir in the vanilla. Divide the batter between two bowls. In a small bowl, mix together the hot coffee and the cocoa, and add this mixture to one of the bowls, creating the chocolate cake batter.

4 Layering the flavors one at a time, scoop or spoon 2 tablespoons of each of the three cake batters into each of the prepared jars. Place the jars 2 inches apart on a large baking sheet. Bake for 20 to 25 minutes, until the centers of the cakes spring back when touched. Remove the cakes from the oven and let them cool completely.

5 While the cakes are baking, make the frosting: Cream the butter, add the confectioners' sugar, and beat thoroughly. Beat in 2 tablespoons of the heavy cream. Divide the frosting into thirds. Add the strawberry puree to one third and mix in. Beat the bittersweet chocolate into the second third and the vanilla extract into the final third. Add a teaspoon or two of additional heavy cream to the buttercream frostings if needed for a smooth consistency.

6 Transfer the three frostings to three piping bags. Cut the tips off to create a ½-inch opening, and then place the three bags into one larger pastry bag fitted with a large star tip. Pipe the frosting onto the cooled cakes in a swirl shape before serving.

caramel crème *cheesecakes*

FOR THE GRAHAM
CRACKER CRUST

FOR THE GRAHAM CRACKER CRUST

Oil for greasing the jars

2 cups graham cracker crumbs

¼ cup sugar

6 tablespoons (¾ stick) unsalted butter, melted

FOR THE CHEESECAKE

3 (8-ounce) packages cream cheese, at room temperature

1 cup sugar

3 large eggs

1 cup sour cream or Greek-style yogurt

2 teaspoons vanilla extract

FOR THE CARAMEL SAUCE

1½ cups sugar

2 tablespoons water

1 teaspoon lemon juice

1½ cups heavy cream

3 tablespoons unsalted butter

MAKES sixteen 4-ounce cheesecakes or eight 8-ounce cheesecakes

There's nothing quite like a simple baked cheesecake. The creamy perfection, smooth with every bite, slides easily over your tongue, all accented with a crisp graham cracker crust. This particular cheesecake keeps things simple—it's topped only with a bit of caramel crème.

———— • ————

1 Preheat the oven to 325°F. Grease the bottoms and sides of sixteen 4-ounce jars or eight 8-ounce jars. Make the crust: In a medium-size bowl, stir together the graham cracker crumbs and the ¼ cup sugar. Stir in the butter and mix until all of the crumbs are coated. Divide the crumb mixture evenly among the jars and use a wine cork or other small, flat-bottomed object to press down into the bottoms of the jars to form the crusts. Set aside.

2 Make the cheesecake: In a large bowl or in a stand mixer, beat the cream cheese until smooth. Add the sugar and beat for 1 minute until incorporated. Scrape down the sides of the bowl and add the eggs one at a time, beating to incorporate after each addition. Mix in the sour cream and vanilla. Spoon or pour the cheesecake filling over the crusts in the jars to ½ inch from the top.

recipe continues

3 Arrange the jars 2 inches apart in high-sided baking pans, such as 9 × 13-inch cake pans, with each pan lined with a clean kitchen towel. Place the pans with the jars in the oven and carefully add hot water to the pans to come halfway up the sides of the jars.

4 Bake the cheesecakes for 20 to 25 minutes, or just until their centers are almost set. Turn off the oven and allow the cheesecakes and water to cool slowly in the oven. When the cheesecakes and water have cooled slightly, remove the pans carefully from the oven and remove the cheesecakes from the pans. Allow to cool completely, cover the jars, and refrigerate for at least 2 hours.

5 Make the caramel sauce: Combine the sugar, water, and lemon juice in a medium-size saucepan over low heat. Cover and cook until the sugar dissolves, about 2 minutes. Increase the heat to medium-high and bring to a boil. Watching closely, boil, stirring occasionally, until the liquid turns golden brown, about 15 minutes. As soon as the color turns, reduce the heat to medium and slowly stir in the cream. The caramel will be hard, but continue cooking until the caramel melts into the cream and the sauce is thick, 3 to 5 minutes. Remove from the heat and stir in the butter. Pour the caramel sauce over the cheesecakes. Serve immediately, or store in the refrigerator until ready to serve.

orange-white chocolate
cheesecakes *with cranberry sauce*

FOR THE CRUST

Oil for greasing the jars

2 cups graham cracker crumbs

¼ cup sugar

6 tablespoons (¾ stick) unsalted butter, melted

FOR THE CHEESECAKE

7 ounces good-quality white chocolate, chopped

½ cup heavy cream

3 (8-ounce) packages cream cheese, at room temperature

¾ cup sugar

4 large eggs

Grated zest of 1 orange

½ teaspoon vanilla extract

½ teaspoon orange extract

Pinch of salt

These creamy white chocolate cheesecakes are flecked with

orange zest and topped with a seasonal cranberry sauce for a dessert designed to grace your table during a holiday gathering.

⸻ • ⸻

1 Preheat the oven to 325°F. Grease the bottoms and sides of sixteen 4-ounce jars or eight 8-ounce jars. Make the crust: In a medium-size bowl, mix together the graham cracker crumbs and ¼ cup sugar. Stir in the butter and mix until all of the crumbs are coated. Divide the crumb mixture evenly among the jars and use a wine cork or other small, flat-bottomed object to press down into the bottoms of the jars to form the crusts. Set aside.

2 Make the cheesecake: Place the white chocolate in a heatproof bowl. In a small saucepan over medium heat, bring the cream just to a boil. Immediately pour the cream over the white chocolate and stir until the chocolate is melted. Set aside.

3 Beat the cream cheese in a stand mixer until smooth, about 3 minutes. Beat in the sugar. Mix in the reserved white chocolate mixture and beat until smooth, scraping down the sides of the bowl as you go. Add the eggs one at a time, beating after each addition. Stir in the orange zest, the vanilla and orange extracts, and the salt. Pour or spoon the cheesecake filling over the crusts in the jars to ½ inch from the top.

recipe continues

FOR THE CRANBERRY SAUCE

12 ounces fresh cranberries

½ cup water

1 cup sugar

Grated zest of 1 orange

MAKES sixteen 4-ounce cheesecakes or eight 8-ounce cheesecakes

4 Arrange the jars 2 inches apart in high-sided baking pans, such as 9 × 13-inch cake pans, with each pan lined with a clean kitchen towel. Place the pans with the jars in the oven and carefully add hot water to the pans to come halfway up the sides of the jars. Bake the cheesecakes for 20 to 25 minutes, or just until their centers are almost set. Turn off the oven and allow the cheesecakes and water to cool slowly in the oven. When the cheesecakes and water have cooled slightly, remove them carefully from the oven and remove the cheesecakes from the pans. Allow to cool completely while making the cranberry topping.

5 Make the cranberry sauce: Place the cranberries, water, and sugar in a large saucepan. Cook over medium-high heat, stirring frequently, until boiling. Reduce the heat to medium-low to simmer, stir in the orange zest, and continue cooking for 7 minutes more. Remove from the heat and allow to cool slightly. Spoon 2 to 3 tablespoons of sauce over the cheesecake in each jar. Transfer the jars to the refrigerator and chill completely before serving. Serve cold.

pumpkin cheesecakes
with a gingersnap crust

FOR THE CRUST

Oil for greasing the jars

3 cups gingersnaps, ground into crumbs

6 tablespoons (¾ stick) unsalted butter, melted

FOR THE CHEESECAKE

3 (8-ounce) packages cream cheese, at room temperature

1½ cups pumpkin puree

1 cup granulated sugar

1 teaspoon ground cinnamon

½ teaspoon ground ginger

¼ teaspoon ground allspice

¼ teaspoon ground cloves

¼ teaspoon freshly grated nutmeg

Pinch of cardamom

3 large eggs

⅓ cup sour cream or Greek-style yogurt

2 teaspoons vanilla extract

When the seasons start to shift and the warm air turns brisk

the world explodes in a fury of pumpkin madness. Whether you're carving them up or baking them into pies, you can't escape the orange orbs of autumn.

———————— • ————————

1 Preheat the oven to 325°F. Grease the bottoms and sides of sixteen 4-ounce jars or eight 8-ounce jars. Make the crust: In a medium-size bowl, mix together the gingersnap crumbs and melted butter until all of the crumbs are coated. Divide the crumb mixture evenly among the jars and use a wine cork or other small, flat-bottomed object to press down into the bottoms of the jars to form the crusts. Set aside.

2 Make the cheesecake: In a large bowl or in a stand mixer, beat the cream cheese until smooth. Beat in the pumpkin puree. Add in the sugar and spices, and beat for 1 minute until incorporated. Scrape down the sides of the bowl and add the eggs one at a time, beating to incorporate after each addition. Mix in the sour cream and vanilla. Spoon or pour the cheesecake filling over the crusts in the jars to ½ inch from the top.

3 Arrange the jars 2 inches apart in high-sided baking pans, such as 9 × 13-inch cake pans, with each pan lined with a clean kitchen towel. Place the pans with the jars in the oven and carefully add hot water to the pans to come halfway up the sides of the jars.

recipe continues

1 cup heavy cream

2 tablespoons confectioners' sugar

Cinnamon, for sprinkling

MAKES sixteen 4-ounce cheesecakes or eight 8-ounce cheesecakes

4 Bake the cheesecakes for 25 to 30 minutes, or just until their centers are almost set. Turn off the oven and allow the cheesecakes and water to cool slowly in the oven for 20 minutes. When the cheesecake and water have cooled slightly, remove them carefully from the oven and remove the cheesecakes from the pans. Allow to cool completely, then cover and refrigerate for at least 2 hours.

5 Before serving, whip together the cream and confectioners' sugar in a bowl until stiff peaks form. Spoon over the tops of the cheesecakes and sprinkle lightly with cinnamon. Serve cold.

flourless chocolate *cakes*

Oil for greasing the jars

7 ounces bittersweet chocolate

4 tablespoons (½ stick) unsalted butter

4 large eggs, separated

1 cup granulated sugar

Confectioners' sugar, for dusting

MAKES 14 individual cakes

You won't even know you're missing the flour with these fudgy cakes. Only a bit of confectioners' sugar is needed for garnish, with the chocolate standing on its own as the star of the show. One bite will have you instantly going back for more.

———————— • ————————

1 Preheat the oven to 350°F. Grease fourteen 8-ounce jars. In a double boiler over simmering water, melt the chocolate and butter until smooth. Remove from the heat and allow to cool slightly. In a separate bowl, use a handheld mixer to beat the egg whites until stiff peaks form. Set aside.

2 In a stand mixer, beat together the granulated sugar and egg yolks until thick and creamy. Mix ¼ cup of the melted chocolate and butter into the egg yolks. Continuing to mix, slowly pour the remaining melted chocolate mixture into the egg yolks until all is incorporated. Fold the egg whites into the chocolate mixture.

3 Spoon 4 to 5 tablespoons of the cake batter into each greased jar. Place the jars 2 inches apart on a large baking sheet. Bake for 25 to 30 minutes, until the tops of the cakes start to crack. Remove from the oven and let the jars cool. Dust with confectioners' sugar before serving. Serve warm or at room temperature.

pull-apart cinnamon breads

12 tablespoons (1½ sticks) unsalted butter, melted

1 cup warm whole milk, at 110°F

⅓ cup warm water, at 110°F

¼ cup granulated sugar

1 package (2¼ teaspoons) instant dry yeast

3 cups all-purpose flour plus ½ cup for rolling the dough

2 teaspoons salt

½ teaspoon ground cardamom

1 cup packed light brown sugar

2 teaspoons ground cinnamon

½ teaspoon ground nutmeg

MAKES 8 individual cinnamon breads

This breakfast-style dessert could adorn any brunch buffet

table. Tiny balls of cardamom-spiced dough are covered in caramelized cinnamon sugar, ready to make you weak in the knees.

———— • ————

1 Grease the bottoms and sides of eight 8-ounce jars with 2 tablespoons of the melted butter. In a stand mixer with the paddle attachment at low speed, mix together the milk, water, granulated sugar, and yeast. Let stand for 5 minutes. Meanwhile, stir together the 3 cups of flour with the salt and cardamom in a separate bowl.

2 Using the dough hook attachment at low speed, slowly add the flour mixture to the yeast mixture. Once all of the flour is in, mix on medium speed for 7 to 8 minutes, until the dough starts to pull into a ball.

3 Sprinkle ¼ cup of flour on a clean, dry work surface and place the dough in the center. Sprinkle an additional 2 to 3 tablespoons of flour over the top of the dough. Knead to form a ball. Place the dough in a greased bowl and cover with a dry cloth. Store in a warm place until the dough has doubled in size, about 1 hour.

4 Punch down the dough. Turn it out onto a floured work surface and roll it into a rectangle. Using kitchen shears or a pizza slicer, cut the dough into 1-inch squares.

5 Mix together the brown sugar, cinnamon, and nutmeg in a medium-size bowl. Dip the dough squares into the remaining melted butter and then roll them gently in the brown sugar mixture. Fill the buttered jars with the dough squares until half full. Set in a warm place to rise for 50 minutes. Meanwhile, preheat the oven to 350°F.

6 Place the jars 2 inches apart on a large baking sheet. Bake the breads for 20 to 25 minutes or until the dough is cooked through. Allow to cool for 5 to 10 minutes. Serve warm.

almond–poppy seed *cakes*

3 tablespoons poppy seeds

2 tablespoons boiling water

1¾ cups all-purpose flour

3 tablespoons cornstarch

2 teaspoons baking powder

1 cup (2 sticks) unsalted butter, softened

1½ cups sugar

4 large egg yolks

4 large eggs

2 teaspoons almond extract

1 teaspoon vanilla extract

¼ cups sliced almonds

MAKES 12 individual almond–poppy seed cakes

This is a dense and moist cake, just begging to be placed at the

brunch dessert table alongside tea or coffee. The poppy seeds provide a slight textural contrast, and you'll find yourself drawn to the perfect simplicity of this cake.

———————— • ————————

1 Place the poppy seeds in a small bowl. Pour the boiling water over them and stir to coat. Allow to sit for 1 hour, stirring halfway through.

2 Preheat the oven to 350°F. Grease twelve 8-ounce jars with butter. Whisk together the flour, cornstarch, and baking powder in a medium-size bowl and set aside. In a large bowl or in a stand mixer, beat the butter and sugar until creamy. In a separate bowl, lightly beat together the egg yolks and eggs. Alternate adding the flour and the eggs to the butter mixture, mixing after each addition. Stir in the almond extract, the vanilla extract, and the moistened poppy seeds.

3 Fill each jar half full with batter and sprinkle with sliced almonds. Place the jars 2 inches apart on a large baking sheet and bake for 25 to 30 minutes, until the tops of the cakes spring back when tapped. Remove from the oven and allow to cool on the baking sheet. Serve warm or at room temperature.

pies and pastries

classic pie dough 42

classic apple pies 45

peach bourbon pies 48

coconut cream pies 51

lemon meringue pies with a
thyme shortbread crust 53

fresh strawberry pies 56

rustic rhubarb custard pies
with a walnut crust 59

profiteroles with
vanilla bean ice cream 60

macarons in a jar 63

pains au chocolat 66

classic pie dough

2½ cups all-purpose flour

1 teaspoon sugar

1 teaspoon salt

1 cup (2 sticks) very cold unsalted butter, cut into ½-inch cubes

4 to 7 tablespoons ice cold water

note: Chilling all your ingredients, even the bowl used to mix your dough, before starting on the pie crust will make the butter slower to melt and will result in a flakier crust.

A good homemade pie crust is a thing of value in your recipe

arsenal. After all, without the crust, pie is just sauced fruit that could take the form of many other desserts. This is a simple and easy recipe, a classic *pâte brisée,* or shortcrust pastry, that turns out a good all-butter crust with little to no hassle.

———————— • ————————

1 In a food processor fitted with the metal blade or in a large bowl using a pastry cutter, mix together the flour, sugar, and salt. Add the butter by dotting pieces of it over the surface of the flour, then pulsing the food processor 2 to 3 times or cutting with the pastry cutter using as few strokes as possible, until pea-sized pieces form.

2 Sprinkle the cold water over the dough and pulse 2 more times, or fold in the water with a fork just enough to wet the dough so the clumps are no longer dry and begin to stick together slightly. Quickly press the dough together with your hands and turn it out onto a large sheet of plastic wrap or parchment paper. Divide the dough into 2 balls and shape the balls into discs. Wrap each disc in plastic wrap or parchment paper and place in the refrigerator for at least 1 hour and up to 2 days.

tips for a perfect pie crust

Making your own pie crust can be a very rewarding experience. Once you get the hang of it, it isn't very difficult at all. However, it can be rather nerve-wracking if you don't have experience with it. Here are a few tips to make your pie crusts turn out well each and every time.

First, keep things cold. The colder the ingredients are, specifically the butter, the easier it will be to get a good pie crust. Warm hands, warm bowls, and a warm environment in general can make the butter melt, which means you won't get that tender pastry dough you're looking for. To make it easier on yourself, chill your mixing bowl or food processor bowl before you start, keep the butter as cold as possible, and don't turn on the oven until after the dough is made and resting in the refrigerator. You can keep a bowl of ice water handy if your hands tend to overheat as you're working. Dipping them in and drying them off periodically will keep them cool and keep that butter firm.

Always let the dough rest. This will give the butter a chance to chill again, and it will also help the dough stick together better. You want the dough to be cold and sticking to itself rather than to your work surface. Avoid over-flouring your work surface. To do this, use a pastry mat or a piece of parchment paper when you roll your dough out. This will help keep it from sticking, and, naturally, you will use less flour as well.

classic
apple pies

1 recipe Classic Pie Dough, page 42

6 cups peeled, cored, and thinly sliced apples, from about 6 medium-size apples

8 tablespoons (1 stick) unsalted butter

¼ cup all-purpose flour

¼ cup granulated sugar

¼ cup packed light or dark brown sugar

1 tablespoon fresh lemon juice

1 teaspoon ground cinnamon

¼ teaspoon freshly grated nutmeg

⅛ teaspoon salt

1 large egg, lightly beaten

3 tablespoons turbinado sugar

MAKES 8 individual apple pies

As much as apple pie has become a piece of Americana,

its origins lie overseas, in places like England, Holland, and Sweden. In one form or another it is still enjoyed the world over.

———————— • ————————

1 Preheat the oven to 350°F. Have ready eight wide-mouth 8-ounce jars. Place 1 of the dough discs on a lightly floured pastry mat or large piece of parchment paper. Roll out the dough to a thickness of ⅛ inch. Cut a 6-inch circle of dough, center it over a jar, and carefully press the dough onto the bottom, up the sides, and over the lip of the jar. Repeat with the remaining seven jars, collecting dough trimmings and rerolling and recutting as necessary.

2 Place the sliced apples in a large heatproof bowl. Melt the butter in a medium-size saucepan over medium-high heat. When the butter is melted, stir in the flour and cook, whisking continuously, until the mixture turns golden brown, about 2 minutes. Add the sugars, lemon juice, cinnamon, nutmeg, and salt, and continue cooking until the mixture comes to a simmer. Remove from the heat and pour over the apples. Toss to coat.

recipe continues

3 Spoon the apple filling into the jars over the pie dough. Roll out the remaining dough disc to a ⅛-inch thickness. Cut eight circles of dough about ½ inch larger than the diameter of the jars. Cover the pies with the dough, trim off the excess dough, crimp the edges to seal, and slice the top to vent. Brush the top crusts with the egg and sprinkle with turbinado sugar.

4 Place the jars 2 inches apart on a large baking sheet. Bake the pies for 45 to 55 minutes, until the crusts are golden brown and the apples are cooked through. Remove from the oven and allow to cool. Serve warm or chilled.

to peel or not to peel

When it comes to fruit desserts, such as apple pie or pear crisps, peeling the fruit is a matter of personal preference. While the recipes in this book will contain a suggestion to peel or not, perhaps you would like to peel when the directions say not to or vice-versa. Does it matter?

In general, the peel left on a fruit serves to add a layer of texture and a bit of bite in the dessert. The peel will not become as soft and cooked through as the fruit that it is encasing, and so there is something still to bite into. Leaving the peel on has the effect of making a dessert feel more rustic. Peeling the fruit, on the other hand, will give the dessert a smoother texture, which you may want. Kids tend to prefer this smoothness.

You may also want to consider where your fruit came from. You might prefer to peel fruits that have been sprayed with pesticides. However, if your fruits are homegrown or organic or you know what was or what was not sprayed on them, the added nutritional benefit of the peel is worth considering.

Whether you choose to peel or not, enjoy your dessert for what it is: dessert. It should be a brilliant encore to your meal that leaves you feeling satisfied and delighted.

peach bourbon *pies*

3 pounds ripe peaches, peeled (see Note), pitted, and cut into 1-inch cubes

½ cup sugar

2 tablespoons cornstarch

2 tablespoons all-purpose flour

2 teaspoons fresh lemon juice

1 tablespoon bourbon

½ teaspoon ground cinnamon

½ teaspoon vanilla extract

1 recipe Classic Pie Dough, page 42

MAKES 8 individual peach pies

note: To peel peaches, make a small X with a knife at the bottom of each peach. Using a slotted spoon, drop each one into a pot of boiling water for 15 seconds. Transfer them immediately to an ice-water bath to stop the cooking. The skin should now peel easily away from the flesh.

As the month of August comes around, the heat of summer

seems unbearable. After surviving July, the thought of another warm and sticky month is overwhelming as you step into the unforgiving sun each day. However, there in the dead of summer the peaches ripen and sing, somehow making that sun seem a little less hot than it did just minutes ago.

You can make this peach pie without the bourbon, instead substituting an extra ½ teaspoon of vanilla extract in its place.

———————— • ————————

1 Preheat the oven to 350°F. In a large bowl, mix together the peaches, sugar, cornstarch, flour, lemon juice, bourbon, cinnamon, and vanilla. Set aside.

2 Have ready eight wide-mouth 8-ounce jars. Place one of the dough discs on a lightly floured pastry mat or large piece of parchment paper. Roll out the dough to a thickness of ⅛ inch. Cut a 6-inch circle of dough, center it over a jar, and carefully press the dough onto the bottom, up the sides, and over the lip of the jar. Repeat with the remaining seven jars, collecting dough trimmings and rerolling and recutting as necessary.

3 Fill each jar generously with the peach mixture. Roll out the remaining dough disc to a ⅛-inch thickness. Cut eight circles of dough about ½ inch larger than the diameter of the jars. Cover the pies with the dough, trim off the excess dough, crimp the

edges to seal, and slice the top to vent. Or, if you like, cut the dough circles into strips, arrange them into lattice crusts, and then crimp the edges to seal.

4 Place the jars 2 inches apart on a large baking sheet. Bake the pies for 50 to 60 minutes, until the crust is golden brown and the filling is thick and bubbly. Cover the tops with aluminum foil if the pies are browning too quickly. Remove from the oven and allow to cool for 30 minutes. Serve warm.

coconut cream
pies

1 recipe Classic Pie Dough, page 42

1 cup unsweetened dried coconut

3¼ cups milk

1 cup granulated sugar

5 large eggs, separated

¼ cup cornstarch

1 tablespoon unsalted butter

2 teaspoons vanilla extract

½ teaspoon coconut extract, optional

MAKES 8 individual coconut cream pies

A creamy coconut pudding sits between a flaky crust on the bottom and a cloud of angelic meringue above. These mini pies won't find their way to the faces of comedians, I hope, but they will make your guests smile.

———————— • ————————

1 Preheat the oven to 350°F. Have ready eight wide-mouth 8-ounce jars. Place one of the dough discs on a lightly floured pastry mat or large piece of parchment paper. (Reserve the other disc for another use.) Roll out the dough to a thickness of ⅛ inch. Using an inverted jar as a cookie cutter, cut eight circles of dough. Place the circles in the bottoms of the jars and press lightly to fit. Place the jars 2 inches apart on a large baking sheet. Bake for 8 to 10 minutes, until the crust is lightly browned. Remove from the oven and allow to cool.

2 In a small bowl, combine the coconut and ¼ cup of the milk. Stir to combine. Set aside to rehydrate the coconut. In a separate heatproof bowl, whisk together ⅔ cup of the sugar with the egg yolks until the mixture is pale yellow and smooth. Set aside.

recipe continues

3 Add the remaining 3 cups milk and the cornstarch to a medium-size saucepan and heat over medium heat until bubbles start to form on the outer edge of the pan. When the milk is hot, slowly pour ½ cup of the milk into the egg yolks while whisking to temper the eggs. Whisk in an additional ½ cup of the milk and then slowly whisk the egg mixture back into the saucepan. Continue cooking over medium heat, stirring continuously, until the mixture thickens and coats the back of the spoon. Remove from the heat and stir in the rehydrated coconut along with the butter, vanilla, and, if you like, the coconut extract. Stir until well incorporated. Spoon the coconut mixture into the jars over the prepared crust. Refrigerate for 3 to 4 hours, until the filling is set.

4 Preheat the oven to 400°F. Remove the jars from the refrigerator and set aside. In a medium-size mixing bowl, use a handheld mixer to beat the egg whites until foamy. Add the remaining ⅓ cup sugar and continue beating until stiff peaks form, to create a meringue. Spoon the meringue over the tops of the coconut creams.

5 Place the jars 2 inches apart on a large baking sheet. Bake the pies for 4 to 5 minutes, until the meringue is golden brown on the peaks. Remove from the oven and allow to cool slightly. Serve immediately, or store in the refrigerator until you are ready to serve them.

lemon meringue
pies *with a thyme shortbread crust*

FOR THE SHORTBREAD CRUST

8 tablespoons (1 stick) unsalted butter, softened

⅓ cup sugar

1 cup all-purpose flour

1 tablespoon cornstarch

2 teaspoons fresh thyme leaves

FOR THE LEMON FILLING

2 cups sugar

½ cup cornstarch

½ teaspoon salt

3 cups water

1 cup fresh lemon juice, from about 4 lemons

Grated zest of 4 lemons

4 tablespoons (½ stick) cold unsalted butter, cut into small pieces

8 large egg yolks, beaten

FOR THE MERINGUE

8 large egg whites

½ cup sugar

MAKES 10 individual lemon meringue pies

Herbed shortbread becomes the crust for this classic lemon

meringue pie, adding a bit of a twist to an old favorite. These tiny treats will win the hearts of the lemon lovers in your life.

—————— • ——————

1 Make the dough for the crusts: Cream together the butter and sugar until light and fluffy, 2 to 3 minutes on medium-high speed. Mix together the flour, cornstarch, and thyme in a separate bowl. Add the flour mixture to the butter mixture and mix until incorporated.

2 Have ready ten wide-mouth 8-ounce jars. Turn out the dough onto a piece of parchment paper. Shape the dough into a long cylinder with a diameter ½ inch smaller than the diameter of the jars you are using. Refrigerate for at least 2 hours.

3 Preheat the oven to 350°F. Slice ¼-inch slices of dough from the roll and place a slice in the bottom of each jar. Place the jars 2 inches apart on a large baking sheet. Bake the crusts for 10 minutes until just lightly golden. Remove from the oven and set aside.

recipe continues

4 Make the filling: Combine the sugar, cornstarch, and salt in a medium-size saucepan. Mix in the water, lemon juice, and lemon zest. Bring to a boil over medium heat, and stir in the butter until it is melted. Place the egg yolks in a heatproof bowl. Slowly pour ½ cup of the lemon mixture into the egg yolks, whisking continuously to temper the eggs. Whisk the egg yolks into the saucepan. Bring to a boil again and continue to cook over medium-high heat until the lemon filling is thick, about 5 minutes. Spoon the filling into the warm jars over the crust.

5 Make the meringue: In a large bowl, beat the egg whites until foamy. Beat in the sugar 1 tablespoon at a time until incorporated. Beat at medium-high speed until stiff peaks form. Spoon or pipe the meringue over the lemon filling in the jars, mounding it in the center to create peaks.

6 Place the jars 2 inches apart on a large baking sheet. Bake the pies for 10 minutes, or just until the meringue is golden brown. Remove from the oven, let cool completely, and chill in the refrigerator for at least 2 hours. Serve cold.

fresh strawberry pies

1 recipe Classic Pie Dough, page 42

3 quarts (12 cups) fresh strawberries, hulled

2 cups sugar

¼ cup cornstarch

1 teaspoon vanilla extract

½ teaspoon salt

Grated zest of 1 lemon

MAKES 12 individual strawberry pies

After a long, cold winter, bright red and juicy strawberries hang from green stems, appearing to bob along to the twinkling beams of sunlight, welcoming them to another season of growing. Celebrate the first berries of the season with a pie as bright and juicy as they are.

———————— • ————————

1 Preheat the oven to 350°F. Have ready twelve wide-mouth 8-ounce jars. Place one of the dough discs on a lightly floured pastry mat or large piece of parchment paper. Roll out the dough to a thickness of ⅛ inch. Cut a 6-inch circle of dough, center it over a jar, and carefully press the dough onto the bottom, up the sides, and over the lip of the jar. Repeat with the remaining eleven jars, using the second dough disc as needed, and collecting dough trimmings and rerolling and recutting as necessary. Crimp or otherwise decorate the top of the crusts if you like.

2 Place a square of parchment paper in each jar to cover the bottom and sides of the jar. Add dry beans or pie weights on top of the parchment. Place the jars 2 inches apart on a large baking sheet. Bake for 10 to 12 minutes, until the crust is golden brown. Remove from the oven and allow to cool on the baking sheet. Remove the parchment paper and beans or pie weights.

3 In a medium-size saucepan combine 1 cup of the strawberries with the sugar, cornstarch, vanilla, and salt. Heat over medium heat until the mixture is bubbling, and then blend together until smooth. (An immersion blender will give you the best results.) Bring to a boil, and boil for 2 minutes. Remove from the heat, stir in the lemon zest, and allow to cool for 10 minutes.

4 Divide the remaining strawberries among the jars, arranging them within the baked crusts. Pour the strawberry sauce over the top of the fresh strawberries until they are covered with a thin layer. Refrigerate at least 4 hours for the strawberries to set up. Serve chilled.

rustic rhubarb
custard pies *with a walnut crust*

FOR THE WALNUT CRUST

3 cups walnuts

2 tablespoons sugar

1 tablespoon ground cinnamon

6 tablespoons (¾ stick) unsalted butter, melted

FOR THE CUSTARD

2 cups sugar

¼ cup all-purpose flour

6 large egg yolks

1 cup heavy cream

4 cups diced rhubarb

MAKES 10 individual custard pies

One of the first plants to spring forth after a long winter,

rhubarb signals the coming of warmer weather. This delightfully tart stalk makes for a pleasant sweet-and-sour pairing in an old-fashioned custard-style pie.

———— • ————

1 Make the crusts: Preheat the oven to 425°F. Place the walnuts, sugar, and cinnamon in a food processor. Pulse several times until the nuts are ground fine. Pour in the butter and pulse until combined. Spoon 2 to 3 tablespoons of the crust mixture into the bottom of each of ten 4-ounce jars and press down lightly.

2 Make the custard: Beat together the sugar, flour, egg yolks, and cream in a bowl until the mixture is thick, creamy, and yellow, about 1 minute. Stir in the rhubarb. Spoon about ⅓ cup of custard into each jar over the walnut crust.

3 Place the jars 2 inches apart on a large baking sheet. Bake the pies for 12 minutes, then reduce the heat to 350°F. Bake for 20 to 22 minutes more, until the custard is set. Remove from the oven and allow to cool. Serve warm, with sweetened whipped cream if you like.

profiteroles with
vanilla bean ice cream

1 cup 2% milk

8 tablespoons (1 stick)
unsalted butter

Pinch of salt

1 cup all-purpose flour

5 large eggs

3 cups vanilla bean ice cream

FOR TOPPING

Chocolate Sauce (recipe,
page 123, or store-bought),
optional

Caramel Sauce (recipe,
page 25, or store-bought),
optional

Strawberry Sauce, optional

MAKES 10 to 12 individual
desserts

Whether you prefer to call them profiteroles, cream puffs, or

choux à la crème, these elegant yet playful little pastries stuffed with ice cream and dipped or drizzled with your choice of sauce are sure to bring a bit of whimsy and fun to your meal.

———————— • ————————

1 Preheat the oven to 375°F. Bring the milk, butter, and salt to a boil in a medium-size saucepan over medium heat. Reduce the heat to low, add the flour, and stir with a wooden spoon to combine into a sticky dough. Continue cooking and stirring the dough for 2 to 3 minutes more, until some of the dough starts to coat the bottom of the pan and the dough is dry.

2 Place the dough in a food processor. Add the eggs one at a time and pulse to incorporate after each addition. Pulse several more times until the dough becomes thick and shiny. Spoon the dough into a pastry bag fitted with a large round tip.

3 Line a large baking sheet with parchment paper. Pipe the dough into mounds about ½ inch smaller in diameter than the 4-ounce jars you are using, leaving at least 2 inches between the mounds. Bake the profiteroles for 20 minutes, or until lightly browned, rotating the sheet 180 degrees halfway through. Turn the oven off and leave the pan in for 10 minutes more.

4 Transfer the profiteroles from the pan to a wire rack and allow to cool completely. Cut each profiterole in half and scoop a small scoop of ice cream into the center. Place in jars. Drizzle with your sauce of choice, or let your guests do so. Serve immediately.

macarons
in a jar

225 grams confectioners' sugar

125 grams almond flour

Vanilla bean seeds scraped from 1 vanilla bean pod

1 teaspoon powdered food coloring or unsweetened cocoa powder, optional

100 grams aged egg whites (from about 3 large eggs; see Note)

25 grams granulated sugar

FOR THE BUTTERCREAM

1 cup (2 sticks) unsalted butter, softened

2 cups confectioners' sugar

1 to 2 tablespoons heavy cream

1 teaspoon vanilla extract

note: Aged egg whites help control moisture levels in the macarons. You can age egg whites by separating the whites from the yolks in advance and then leaving the whites in a bowl, partially covered, in a cool place for up to 2 days.

These French cookies can be found just about everywhere

these days. They're the perfect treats to tuck into jars for guests to enjoy right away or to take home as party favors. Your choices for flavors and colors are endless, and can be changed to match the theme of your party, your sports team, or simply your flavor cravings. Perhaps you want green cookies on the bottom of your jar? No problem at all. Green bottoms there shall be.

The best macaron recipes use gram measurements for a higher degree of accuracy. All you need is a kitchen scale with the gram option, which the majority of them have, and you're all set to bake macarons at home.

———— • ————

1 Make the macarons: Place the confectioners' sugar, almond flour, and vanilla bean seeds into a food processor and pulse until well combined. If you like, add food coloring or cocoa powder. Set aside. In a stand mixer with a whisk attachment, beat the egg whites until they are foamy. Add the granulated sugar and continue beating until the mixture forms peaks and has the appearance and consistency of a shiny shaving cream. Do not overbeat.

recipe continues

2 Sift the almond mixture into the egg whites and fold with a wooden spoon to combine until the batter recedes back into itself within 10 seconds when the spoon is lifted out. Use no more than 50 strokes, to avoid overworking the batter.

3 Place the batter in a large piping bag fitted with a large or extra-large round tip. Pinch the end when filling so that the macaron batter does not run out. Pipe small circles 1 to 1½ inches in diameter onto baking sheets lined with silicone baking sheets or parchment paper. Allow the circles to rest for at least 30 minutes.

4 Preheat the oven to 280°F. Bake the macaron shells for 15 to 20 minutes, until they are cooked through and dry to a light touch. Remove from the oven and allow to cool on the pan for 10 minutes. If the shells are not to be filled immediately, store them in airtight containers in the refrigerator for up to 5 days.

5 Make the buttercream: Cream the butter for 2 minutes. Add the confectioners' sugar and mix thoroughly. Mix in 1 tablespoon of the heavy cream and the vanilla. Add 1 to 2 more teaspoons of cream if necessary to get a smooth consistency.

6 Pipe or carefully spread the buttercream onto the bottom side of one shell, then top with a second shell. Carefully fill jars of desired size with macarons and serve.

how to create your own layered desserts

There are several layered desserts in this book, such as the Banana Buttermilk Trifles, page 107, and the Peach-Raspberry Verrines with Lemon-Thyme Cream, page 98. Jars lend themselves well to these kinds of desserts, where each layer showcases a different ingredient.

It's rather simple to create your own trifles and verrines in jars, and the presentation is very attractive. Here are a few guidelines for ingredients:

CAKES: Cut or cubed cakes are used in trifles. Consider a cake sprinkled or misted with alcohol to infuse flavor into the dessert.

COOKIES: Whether crumbled, broken, or whole, cookies add texture to a layered dessert.

CREAMS: Creamy layers act as the glue that holds it all together. Puddings, custards, and yogurts in a variety of flavors are all good choices.

FRUIT: Use slices of larger fruits or small berries in their whole form. You can also top layered desserts with a fruit sauce or syrup.

Here are some specific ideas to get you started:

"DIRT CUPS" FOR KIDS: Layers of chocolate cookies, chocolate pudding, and gummy worms are always a kid favorite.

PIÑA COLADA TRIFLE: Rum-soaked pound cake, coconut pudding, pineapple chunks, whipped cream, and toasted coconut would be perfect for a backyard luau.

pains *au chocolat*

¾ cup whole milk

1 tablespoon instant dry yeast

2 cups all-purpose flour

3 tablespoons sugar

1 teaspoon salt

1 cup (2 sticks) cold unsalted butter, cut into chunks

6 ounces good-quality semisweet chocolate, cut with a sharp knife into 16 long, thin pieces

MAKES 8 individual *pains au chocolat*

Bread and chocolate: Smooth, velvety chocolate is hugged by

layers of flaky dough, waiting to be discovered. For me, making this dough, which requires multiple turns of rolling and chilling the dough, is a labor of love. You end up with buttery layers that seem to melt in your mouth the moment they hit your tongue. If you have the persistence, this is a dish that pays off tenfold. Plan ahead and freeze the dough in advance, if you like.

———————— • ————————

1 Pour the milk into a small bowl and stir in the yeast to bloom. In the bowl of a stand mixer, mix 1½ cups of the flour with the sugar and salt. Add the yeast mixture to the bowl of the mixer and mix to combine.

2 In a stand mixer with the dough hook attached, mix the dough for about 5 minutes until it pulls away from the sides of the bowl, adding a tablespoon of flour if necessary if the dough is too wet. Form into a rectangle about 7 × 10 inches in size and place on a parchment paper–lined baking sheet. Cover with plastic wrap and place in the refrigerator for 1 hour.

3 While the dough is chilling, toss the butter with 2 tablespoons of flour. Press the floured butter between 2 pieces of parchment paper into a 5-inch square, using the parchment to guide the butter.

note: If you're pressed for time, you can also use frozen prepared puff pastry sheets. Simply thaw sheets as directed in the package, unfold, cut to the size indicated in step 6, and proceed with the recipe.

4 Turn the dough out onto a lightly floured work surface and roll it into a 10-inch square. Place the butter square diagonally on top of the dough square, so that the corners of the butter square are centered along the sides of the dough square. Fold the 4 dough corners toward the center of the butter and pinch to seal, completely enclosing the butter. Turn the dough over and begin rolling the dough from one side, slowly at first, just tapping the square with the rolling pin until the butter softens enough to roll, and dusting with flour as you go to keep the dough from sticking. Roll the dough into a rectangle about 7 × 10 inches in size, and then fold the short ends of the dough to meet in the center, creating the appearance of an open book. Fold again at the center, as if closing the book. Fold the dough into thirds. Cover the dough in plastic wrap and chill it in the refrigerator for 2 hours.

5 Once the dough is chilled, unwrap it and roll it into a long rectangle. Fold again into thirds, rotate the dough 90 degrees, then roll out again into a long rectangle. Fold the long rectangle into thirds once more, forming a square. Press down lightly and wrap in plastic wrap. Chill for 2 hours. Repeat this process twice more. At this point, you can freeze the dough for later use.

recipe continues

6 After the final chilling time, preheat the oven to 400°F. Roll the dough out on a lightly floured surface to create a 14- or 15-inch square. Let the dough rest for 5 minutes. Cut the dough in half down the center using a pizza cutter or pastry roller, then cut it in half again the opposite way to create 4 squares. Cut each square down the center to form 8 rectangles.

7 Place a piece of chocolate near the short edge of each rectangle, then fold that end of the dough over and seal the chocolate in. Near the edge of that seal, place another piece of chocolate and roll again, continuing to roll until you reach the end of the rectangle. Set aside. Repeat with the remaining 7 dough rectangles.

8 Pinch together one of the open sides of each roll to seal in the chocolate. Place this sealed end in the bottom of a 4-ounce jar. Repeat with seven more jars. Arrange the jars 2 inches apart on a large baking sheet. Place the baking sheet in the oven and bake for 15 to 20 minutes, until the dough is puffed and golden brown. Remove from the oven and allow to cool on the baking sheet. Serve warm or at room temperature.

custards _and_ puddings

lemon–sour cream mousse 72

espresso crèmes brûlées 74

dark chocolate–hazelnut
pots de crème 77

white chocolate–lime
puddings 80

lemon-blueberry
bread puddings 83

indian rice puddings 84

sweet corn panna cotta with
bacon & blueberry sauce 87

peanut butter & jelly
parfaits 88

lemon-sour cream
mousse

2 tablespoons plus ¾ cup water

1 tablespoon fresh lemon juice

1 (¼-ounce) envelope unflavored gelatin

1½ cups sour cream

4 ounces cream cheese, softened

Grated zest of ½ lemon

¾ cup sugar

1 cup heavy cream

Fresh berries, such as raspberries or blueberries, for garnish

MAKES 6 individual desserts

Eating this mousse is like biting into clouds of citrus-flecked

cream. It is great for a light and airy finish to a summer meal or to follow up a heavier dish any time of year. Serve it alongside seasonal berries for bursts of sweet to complement the tangy lemon.

———————— • ————————

1 Combine the 2 tablespoons water and lemon juice in a bowl and sprinkle the gelatin over the top. Let rest for 5 minutes.

2 In a medium-size mixing bowl, beat together the sour cream, cream cheese, and lemon zest until fluffy.

3 In a small saucepan, heat the remaining ¾ cup water and ½ cup of the sugar over medium heat, stirring frequently, until the sugar is completely dissolved. Remove from the heat and pour into the gelatin, stirring until completely dissolved. Add the gelatin mixture to the sour cream mixture and beat together until well incorporated.

4 In a separate bowl, whip the heavy cream with the remaining ¼ cup of sugar using a handheld mixer until stiff peaks form. Fold the whipped cream into the sour cream mixture. Spoon into six 4-ounce jars, cover, and chill in the refrigerator until firm, about 2 hours. Spoon the berries over the top and serve.

espresso crèmes brûlées

1 quart heavy cream

Vanilla bean seeds scraped from 1 vanilla bean pod

½ cup granulated sugar

8 large egg yolks

1 teaspoon finely ground espresso beans

¼ cup vanilla turbinado sugar (see Note)

MAKES 10 individual *crèmes brûlées*

note: Vanilla sugar is sugar made by adding vanilla seeds and dried vanilla bean pods to granulated sugar or turbinado sugar (I prefer the latter) and allowing them to sit together for weeks until the vanilla flavor is infused into the sugar. In this recipe, you can substitute unflavored turbinado sugar or granulated sugar if you don't have access to vanilla sugar.

This classic cream custard is given a bit of a bump with finely

ground espresso. You create a thin, crisp caramel layer with help from your friendly blowtorch, and dessert is served, jar style.

———— • ————

1 Preheat the oven to 300°F. Place the cream and the vanilla bean seeds and pod in a medium-size saucepan. Bring the mixture just to a boil and turn off the heat. Cover and allow to cool for 5 to 10 minutes.

2 In a separate bowl, lightly beat together the granulated sugar and egg yolks. Remove the vanilla bean pod from the cream mixture and slowly whisk the cream into the egg yolks. Whisk until the mixture is smooth and the sugar is dissolved. Stir in the espresso. Strain the mixture through a sieve to remove any lumps.

3 Fill ten 4-ounce jars with the cream mixture. Place the jars 1 to 2 inches apart in a high-sided baking pan lined with a clean towel. Place the pan in the oven. Carefully pour hot water into the pan, taking care not to get any water in the jars, until the water is halfway up the sides of the jars. Bake for 50 to 55 minutes, until the custard is just set but still has some wiggle in the center.

4 Remove the jars from the water bath and let cool slightly. Transfer them to the refrigerator and refrigerate until completely chilled, 2 to 3 hours.

5 To serve, remove the custards from the refrigerator and gently dry off any condensation that may have collected on the tops of the custards. Distribute the vanilla sugar among the 10 custards. Tilt the jars to cover the tops of the custards completely. Using a kitchen torch, heat the sugar until it turns golden brown. Allow to sit at least 5 minutes before serving. Serve chilled.

dark chocolate–hazelnut
pots de crème

FOR THE CUSTARD

4 ounces bittersweet chocolate (70% cacao)

2 cups heavy cream

½ cup whole milk

4 large egg yolks

1 large egg

¼ cup granulated sugar

2 teaspoons hazelnut liqueur

FOR THE TOPPING

1 cup heavy cream

2 tablespoons confectioners' sugar

1 teaspoon hazelnut liqueur

¼ cup toasted hazelnuts

MAKES 6 *pots de crème*

Dark, rich chocolate meets toasted hazelnut in this soft

custard dessert. It's an elegant treat that would be the perfect end to a sit-down dinner with friends or served blanket-side at a picnic in the park.

• ────

1 Preheat the oven to 320°F. Line a 9 × 13-inch metal baking pan with a towel.

2 Make the custard: Break up the bittersweet chocolate into chunks and put it in a double boiler over simmering water. Stir and heat until the chocolate is just melted. Turn off the heat and set aside.

3 In a thick-bottomed medium-size saucepan, combine the cream and milk. Scald the mixture over medium heat, stirring frequently, until small bubbles form on the outside of the surface of the cream and the temperature reaches 185°F on an instant-read thermometer. Remove from the heat.

4 In a medium-size bowl, beat together the egg yolks, whole egg, and granulated sugar until the sugar is dissolved. Slowly temper the eggs by pouring a slow stream of the hot scalded cream mixture into them while whisking constantly. Then whisk the tempered egg mixture into the cream mixture. Whisk in the melted chocolate and continue whisking until all of the chocolate is incorporated into the mixture. Stir in the hazelnut liqueur.

recipe continues

5 Pour the chocolate mixture into six 4- to 6-ounce jars until the jars are filled to within ½ inch from the top. Place the filled jars in the prepared pan. Place the pan in the oven and then carefully pour hot water into the pan to reach halfway up the sides of the jars.

6 Bake for 30 to 35 minutes, until the outside edges of the custards are set but the centers still jiggle. Allow to cool at room temperature, then chill in the refrigerator for at least 2 hours.

7 Make the topping: Just before serving, beat the cream, confectioners' sugar, and hazelnut liqueur together until soft peaks form. Spoon the whipped cream over the tops of the custards, sprinkle with toasted hazelnuts, and serve.

how to clean jars

Because of their small size, jars can be a bit difficult to clean if you end up with cake or cookie stuck in the bottom and your hand doesn't fit. Not to worry, though, there are plenty of ways to get it out without elbow grease.

First, after the jars are empty, soak them in a tub of warm soapy water. This will help soften any dessert pieces that may be stuck inside and get the water to do some of the washing for you. Next, run them through your dish-washer or wash them as you would any cup or bottle by hand. A bottle brush will come in handy here for extremely small jars or jars with a lip.

how to fill a pastry bag

There are several recipes within the pages of this book that recommend the use of a pastry bag. It's a handy tool, especially when filling jars, because it allows you to get your filling down into the jar and put it exactly where you want it.

Filling a pastry bag can be something of a mystery if you have not done it before. How do the contents of this bowl make their way into that collapsible bag? There is a quick and easy way to get the job done.

If you are using a decorator's tip rather than cutting the end of the bag, put the tip in place prior to filling the bag. Twist the bag just behind the tip, or use a twist tie to close off the opening and to keep the batter or frosting from leaking as you fill. Then, simply place the pastry bag in a pint glass or other tall glass, folding the wide end of the bag over the edge of the glass, which will hold the bag open. Now you can spoon your dessert filling into the bag easily.

When you're finished, remove the bag from the glass, twist the wide end of the bag to seal it, and then remove the twist tie when you're ready to fill the jars.

white chocolate–lime
puddings

2/3 cup sugar

3 tablespoons cornstarch

1/8 teaspoon salt

1 cup heavy cream

2 cups whole milk

4 large egg yolks

6 ounces white chocolate, melted and cooled slightly

Grated zest of 1 lime

1 tablespoon unsalted butter

MAKES 6 individual puddings

Pudding isn't just for kids anymore when creamy white

chocolate enters the picture, but you may have to fight them for it. These delightful jars are filled with a thick pudding that will make you feel like a kid again. I'll take one in my lunchbox, please.

———————— • ————————

1 Sift together the sugar, cornstarch, and salt into a medium-size saucepan. Slowly whisk in the cream and the milk. Beat together the egg yolks and add to the melted chocolate. Whisk the chocolate mixture into the saucepan along with the lime zest. Heat over medium-high heat, stirring constantly, just until the mixture comes to a boil. Lower the heat to medium-low and cook, stirring constantly, for about 2 minutes, until the pudding thickly coats the back of a wooden spoon. Remove from the heat and stir in the butter.

2 Pour the pudding through a sieve to remove any lumps. Spoon into six 4- to 6-ounce jars. Cover and refrigerate for at least 2 hours, until cooled and thickened. Serve chilled.

lemon-blueberry
bread puddings

1 pound rustic artisan bread, crusts included

4 large eggs

1 cup sugar

½ cup mascarpone cheese

3 cups whole milk

2 teaspoons vanilla extract

Grated zest of 1 lemon

1 teaspoon fresh lemon juice

3 tablespoons unsalted butter, melted

1½ cups blueberries, fresh or frozen

¾ cup heavy cream

2 teaspoons agave nectar

MAKES 12 individual puddings

Blueberry season is a favorite here in the Midwest. The thick air and heat of summer have given way to a breezy warm sunshine that hints at the fall to come, and with the evening air cooling fast, warm desserts again become a welcome end to a summer's day. This bread pudding is bursting with the season's finest berries, brightened with a bit of lemon for a late summer delight.

—————— • ——————

1 Preheat the oven to 350°F. Grease twelve 8-ounce jars. Cut the bread into 1½-inch cubes, place in a large bowl, and set aside.

2 In a large bowl, beat the eggs and mix in the sugar and mascarpone. Add the milk, vanilla, lemon zest, and lemon juice and beat until evenly combined. Stir in the melted butter.

3 Pour the milk and egg mixture over the bread cubes and stir until all the pieces of bread are completely soaked. Allow the bread to sit for 20 minutes.

4 Stir the blueberries into the pudding mixture and immediately spoon into the jars, filling each only half full. Place the jars on a large baking sheet 2 inches apart. Bake for 30 to 35 minutes, until the tops of the puddings are evenly browned. Remove from the oven, set on a clean, dry towel, and let rest 15 to 20 minutes. Just before serving, pour the cream and agave nectar into a lidded jar and shake to combine. Drizzle over the top of the bread puddings and serve.

indian
rice puddings

½ teaspoon unsalted butter

½ cup basmati rice

3½ cups whole milk

½ cup heavy cream

3 heaping tablespoons sugar

½ teaspoon freshly ground green cardamom

2 tablespoons sliced almonds

2 tablespoons hulled pistachios

2 tablespoons golden raisins

MAKES 10 individual puddings

This simple, traditional dish is a staple at Indian celebrations, much like pumpkin pie for Thanksgiving in the United States. While *kheer* is the name of any sort of Indian sweet pudding, it is often this rice pudding to which it refers.

———————— • ————————

1 In a heavy-bottomed medium saucepan, heat the butter over medium-high heat until melted. Add the rice and sauté for 2 minutes, stirring constantly. Add the milk and cream. Bring the mixture to a boil, reduce the heat to medium-low, and continue cooking, stirring occasionally, for 20 to 30 minutes, until the rice is cooked through but not mushy. There will be more liquid left in the pan than there usually is when you cook rice.

2 Stir in the sugar, cardamom, almonds, and 1 tablespoon of the pistachios. Simmer for 5 minutes, stirring occasionally. Remove from the heat and allow to cool slightly. Pour the pudding into ten 8-ounce jars, filling them to within ½ inch from the top. Garnish with the remaining pistachios and the raisins and allow to continue cooling. Serve warm, or place completely cooled puddings in the refrigerator and serve chilled.

sweet corn panna cotta *with bacon & blueberry sauce*

FOR THE PANNA COTTA

3 tablespoons cold water

1 (¼-ounce) envelope unflavored gelatin

¾ cup whole milk

3 ears sweet corn, husked, with kernels removed from cob

¼ cup sugar

1 cup heavy cream

FOR THE BACON AND BLUEBERRY SAUCE

3 strips thick-sliced bacon, coarsely chopped

1 cup blueberries

½ cup sugar

MAKES 6 individual panna cotta desserts

Here is a nod to the Midwest, where my roots lie and where

rows of sweet corn grow all summer long, tall and beautiful. This creamy cup is topped with fresh seasonal blueberries and a bit of salty bacon to complete the circle. Here in middle America, we pair bacon and blueberries with our corn. You should, too.

———————— • ————————

1 Make the panna cotta: Pour the cold water into a large bowl and sprinkle the gelatin over the top. Set aside.

2 In a medium-size saucepan over medium heat, combine the milk, corn, and sugar. Bring to a simmer and simmer for 5 minutes without boiling. Remove from the heat and let cool slightly. Pour the mixture into a blender, pulse until smooth, and strain through cheesecloth back into the saucepan. Add the cream, heat over medium heat, and simmer for 10 minutes.

3 Pour the cream mixture over the gelatin. Stir until all the gelatin is dissolved. Pour into six 4-ounce jars. Cover and refrigerate for 4 hours, or overnight, until the panna cotta is firm.

4 Make the sauce: In a medium-size frying pan over medium heat, fry the bacon pieces until crisp. Remove the bacon using a slotted spoon and drain on paper towels. Add the blueberries and sugar to the bacon grease in the pan. Continue to cook over medium heat, stirring frequently, until a thick sauce forms. Remove from the heat.

5 Spoon the blueberry sauce over the chilled panna cotta. Sprinkle with the bits of bacon. Serve immediately.

peanut butter & jelly *parfaits*

FOR THE VANILLA CAKE

¾ cup all-purpose flour

½ cup sugar

¾ teaspoon baking powder

¼ teaspoon salt

4 tablespoons (½ stick) unsalted butter, softened

⅓ cup sour cream

1 large egg

1 teaspoon vanilla extract

FOR THE PEANUT BUTTER MOUSSE

2 cups creamy peanut butter

1 cup confectioners' sugar

3 cups heavy cream

3 cups good-quality seeded raspberry preserves

FOR THE WHIPPED TOPPING

1 cup heavy cream

2 tablespoons confectioners' sugar

2 cups fresh raspberries

1 cup roasted salted or unsalted peanuts

MAKES 18 individual parfaits

A bit of raspberry and a creamy peanut butter mousse, made

perfect with the addition of a sweet vanilla cake. Who says the sandwiches of our youth can't be transformed into sophisticated desserts? This layered nod to the lunchbox will take away any prejudices you have about peanut butter and jelly pairings, and soon you'll be playing hopscotch and waiting for the bell to ring.

———————————— • ————————————

1 Make the vanilla cake: Preheat the oven to 350°F. Line a muffin tin with 6 paper or foil liners. In a medium bowl, whisk together the flour, sugar, baking powder, and salt. In a stand mixer, beat the butter until creamy, about 2 minutes. Add the sour cream and mix until incorporated. Mix in the egg and stir in the vanilla. Slowly add the flour mixture in three separate parts until just mixed.

2 Scoop the batter into the muffin liners, filling ⅔ full. Bake for 20 to 22 minutes, or until the tops are golden brown. Remove from the oven and transfer to a wire rack to cool completely.

3 Make the peanut butter mousse: In a large mixing bowl, beat the peanut butter and confectioners' sugar together until creamy, 2 to 3 minutes. Slowly mix in 2 cups of the heavy cream until incorporated. In a separate bowl, beat the remaining 1 cup cream until stiff peaks form. Fold the whipped cream into the peanut butter mixture and put in the refrigerator to chill.

note: The cupcakes can be made ahead of time. Or you can use your favorite cupcake or leftover cupcakes for the cake slices that go between the peanut butter and the jelly.

4 In a small saucepan, bring the raspberry preserves to a boil over medium-high heat. Remove from the heat and allow to cool slightly. Spoon 2 to 3 tablespoons into the bottom of eighteen 4- or 6-ounce jars. Allow to cool further.

5 Remove the vanilla cupcakes from their liners and slice cross-wise into thirds. Layer one cake round over the jam. Using a pastry bag, or by spooning carefully, add a 1½- to 2-inch layer of peanut butter mousse to each jar.

6 Make the whipped topping: In a medium bowl, beat together the cream and the confectioners' sugar until stiff peaks form. Spoon a thin layer of whipped cream over each jar. Top with the fresh raspberries and peanuts. Chill until ready to serve.

fruit desserts

apple pancake puffs 93

cardamom pear crisps 94

cherry-almond crumbles 97

peach-raspberry verrines
with lemon-thyme cream 98

rosemary-peach cobblers 100

strawberry shortcakes 102

ginger mascarpone with
caramelized apricots 104

banana buttermilk trifles 107

sparkling pomegranate
& orange jelly cups 110

apple
pancake puffs

3 medium-size apples, cored, peeled, and sliced

3 tablespoons granulated sugar

2 tablespoons unsalted butter

2 teaspoons fresh lemon juice

¼ teaspoon ground cinnamon

FOR THE PANCAKE PUFFS

4 large eggs

1 cup whole milk

1 cup all-purpose flour

¼ teaspoon salt

4 tablespoons (½ stick) unsalted butter

Confectioners' sugar, for topping

MAKES 6 individual pancake puffs

Often called "Dutch babies" or "German pancakes," these little pancakes are sure to make you smile. With an almost pie-like filling and a puffed, bready crust, they are an instant hit with kids and adults alike.

———————— • ————————

1 Make the apple topping: Combine the apples, granulated sugar, 2 tablespoons butter, lemon juice, and cinnamon in a medium-size saucepan. Cover and simmer over medium-low heat until the apples are just starting to soften, 5 to 10 minutes. Remove from the heat and set aside.

2 Make the pancake puffs: Preheat the oven to 375°F. Beat together the eggs and milk in a bowl. Add the flour and salt and whisk until the batter is smooth.

3 Distribute the butter equally among six wide-mouth 8-ounce jars. Arrange the jars 2 inches apart on a large baking sheet. Place the baking sheet with the jars in the oven for 2 to 3 minutes, just to melt the butter. Spoon the apple topping into the jars, distributing equally. Pour the batter over the apple topping. Bake for 25 to 30 minutes, until the edges of the pancakes are a light golden brown. Remove from the oven and let cool slightly on the baking sheet. Dust with confectioners' sugar, and serve immediately.

cardamom pear *crisps*

FOR THE PEAR FILLING

20 small pears, such as Forelle or Seckel varieties, or 10 medium-size pears, such as Anjou

Juice of 1 lemon

¼ cup granulated sugar

2 tablespoons cornstarch

¼ teaspoon ground cinnamon

FOR THE CRISP TOPPING

½ cup all-purpose flour

½ cup rolled oats

½ cup packed dark brown sugar

½ teaspoon ground cardamom (see Note)

½ teaspoon ground ginger

Pinch of salt

8 tablespoons (1 stick) unsalted butter, softened

MAKES 6 individual crisps

note: For the most fragrant cardamom flavor, buy green cardamom pods, remove the seeds, and grind the seeds in a mortar and pestle or in a clean coffee grinder.

Sometimes overlooked for their crisp apple counterparts, pears

work exceptionally well in desserts, their buttery and velvety flesh lending itself to spiced pairings and hearty baked toppings. Curl up with a warm jar of freshly baked pear crisp on a brisk autumn eve, and you'll forget all about those red orbs.

1 Make the filling: Preheat the oven to 350°F. Core the pears and cut them into ¼-inch slices. Put the pear slices in a large bowl. Add the lemon juice and toss gently to coat the pears and keep them from browning. Mix in the sugar, cornstarch, and cinnamon. Fill six 8-ounce jars with the pears to ¼ inch from the top. Although ¼ inch might seem like too little room for the topping, note that the pears will cook down and some of the topping will drip down in between the pears.

2 Make the topping: In a separate bowl, stir together the flour, oats, brown sugar, cardamom, ginger, and salt to mix well. Add the butter and use a fork to incorporate it into the dry ingredients until the mixture is crumbly.

3 Spoon the topping over the pears to cover, and use the back of the spoon to pack the topping down tightly. Place the jars 2 inches apart on a large baking sheet. Bake for 25 to 30 minutes, until the pears are cooked through and the topping is light golden brown. Remove from the oven and let cool slightly on the baking sheet. Serve warm.

cherry-almond crumbles

FOR THE CRUMBLE

1½ cups all-purpose flour

½ cup sugar

½ teaspoon baking powder

⅛ teaspoon salt

1 large egg

4 ounces almond paste

½ teaspoon almond extract

8 tablespoons (1 stick) cold unsalted butter, cut into pieces

½ cup sliced almonds

FOR THE FILLING

5 cups sweet cherries, pitted and halved

¼ cup sugar

2 teaspoons cornstarch

MAKES 9 individual crumbles

There's something magical about fresh fruit still hanging

on the trees, sitting in the warm sun. Succulent red cherries are front and center in this simple dessert, accompanied by a light almond crumble. You can almost envision plucking the cherries off the trees and plopping them down directly into the jars you're eating from, bite after bite.

———— • ————

1 Make the crumble: Preheat the oven to 350°F. In a food processor or in a bowl using a pastry cutter, mix together the flour, sugar, baking powder, salt, egg, almond paste, and almond extract. Add the butter pieces and pulse or use a fork to mix until the mixture is crumbly. Press 3 rounded tablespoons of the mixture into the bottoms of 9 wide-mouth 8-ounce jars.

2 Make the filling: In a separate bowl, mix together the cherries, sugar, and cornstarch. Divide the cherry mixture among the jars, filling each jar to just below the lip. Mix the sliced almonds with the remaining crumble and add 3 rounded tablespoons of crumble to each jar to cover the cherries. Pack the crumble mixture down lightly to keep it in place.

3 Place the jars 2 inches apart on a large baking sheet. Bake for 25 minutes, or until the tops of the crumbles start to turn golden brown. Remove from the oven and let cool on the baking sheet. Serve warm or cold.

peach-raspberry
verrines with lemon-thyme cream

FOR THE LEMON-THYME CREAM

5 large egg yolks

¾ cup sugar

Grated zest of 4 lemons, plus ½ cup fresh lemon juice squeezed from about 2 of them

3 fresh thyme sprigs

6 tablespoons (¾ stick) unsalted butter, softened

1 cup heavy cream

FOR THE PEACH-RASPBERRY VERRINES

4 to 6 ripe peaches

1 cup fresh raspberries

8 fresh thyme sprigs, for garnish

MAKES 8 individual verrines

Just when summer starts to become unbearably hot, when

the air is thick and the sun is unforgiving, there is a sudden burst of flavor that springs forth from the earth. Peaches turn golden on the trees, berries blush, and green is everywhere. Celebrating the freshest tastes of summer, peaches and raspberries are layered here between layers of cool lemon cream, an elegantly simple dessert to cool and refresh on a hot summer day. For a shortcut, you can use 1 cup of store-bought lemon curd rather than making your own.

———— • ————

1 Make the lemon-thyme cream: Whisk together the egg yolks in a medium-size bowl and set aside. In a medium-size saucepan, heat the sugar, lemon zest, lemon juice, and 3 thyme sprigs over medium heat until the sugar completely dissolves and the mixture begins to simmer just slightly around the edges.

2 Whisk in the butter 1 tablespoon at a time until incorporated. Temper the egg yolks by whisking 2 tablespoons of the hot liquid into the yolks. Slowly pour the tempered yolks into the saucepan, whisking constantly. Heat, stirring, until the mixture thickens and coats the back of a wooden spoon. Remove from the heat, remove and discard the thyme sprigs, and allow to cool completely. Refrigerate the lemon curd overnight.

3 Whip the heavy cream until stiff peaks form. Whisk the chilled lemon curd and then fold in the whipped cream until incorporated.

4 Make the verrines: Thinly slice the peaches and squeeze some lemon juice over the pieces to prevent browning. Fan out the slices in the bottoms of eight 8-ounce jars. Spoon 2 to 3 tablespoons of lemon cream over the peaches. Add a single layer of raspberries, then spoon another 2 to 3 tablespoons of lemon cream over the top of those. Finish with a fan of peaches and a sprig of fresh thyme. Serve cool.

rosemary-peach cobblers

FOR THE PEACH FILLING

4 cups peeled and sliced peaches

½ cup sugar

2 tablespoons water

1 tablespoon fresh lemon juice

2 sprigs rosemary, bruised

4 tablespoons (½ stick) unsalted butter, melted

FOR THE CRUST TOPPING

1 cup all-purpose flour

1½ cups sugar

1 teaspoon baking powder

1 teaspoon grated lemon zest

¼ teaspoon salt

4 tablespoons (½ stick) cold unsalted butter, cut into pieces

1 cup whole milk

MAKES 8 individual peach cobblers

A hint of rosemary adds depth and complexity to a classic Southern favorite. Perfectly round peaches and a biscuit-like crumble bake together, melding their flavors and becoming one. Then they are topped by a creamy layer of ice cream that melts into the cracks and crevices. You can bruise rosemary in a mortar and pestle (tap the leaves, but don't pulverize them), or use a mallet or the back of a knife on a cutting board.

———————— • ————————

1 Make the filling: In a large saucepan, combine the peaches, sugar, water, lemon juice, and rosemary over medium-high heat. Bring to a boil, lower the heat, and simmer for 10 minutes, or until a sauce starts to thicken around the peaches. Remove from the heat and set aside.

2 Preheat the oven to 350°F. Evenly distribute the melted butter among eight 8-ounce jars. Make the topping: Mix together the flour, sugar, baking powder, lemon zest, and salt in a food processor. Add the cold butter and pulse just until the dough starts to form coarse crumbs.

3 Pour the dough into a medium-size bowl and stir in the milk just until combined. Distribute the dough mixture on top of the butter in the jars.

4 Remove the rosemary sprigs from the peaches and spoon approximately ⅔ cup peaches and sauce into each jar on top of the dough. Place the jars 2 inches apart on a large baking sheet. Bake for 30 to 35 minutes, until the crust starts to brown.

5 Remove from the oven and allow the jars to rest on the baking sheet for at least 20 minutes before serving. Serve warm or cold.

strawberry *shortcakes*

4 cups strawberries, hulled and thinly sliced

¼ cup granulated sugar

FOR THE BISCUITS

2 cups all-purpose flour

3 tablespoons granulated sugar, plus more for sprinkling

2 tablespoons baking powder

½ teaspoon salt

Grated zest of 1 lemon

7 tablespoons cold unsalted butter, cut into small pieces, plus 2 tablespoons melted butter

1½ cups heavy cream

FOR THE WHIPPED CREAM

1 cup heavy cream

1 tablespoon confectioners' sugar

Mint sprigs for garnish, optional

MAKES 6 to 8 individual strawberry shortcakes

This classic dessert was immortalized for an entire

generation by a red-headed, strawberry-scented character. Here it is presented tucked into a jar for a portable treat that makes you want to enjoy it atop a blanket on a grassy hillside.

———— • ————

1 Put the strawberries in a bowl and sprinkle with the granulated sugar. Set aside to macerate.

2 Make the biscuits: Mix together the flour, the 3 tablespoons granulated sugar, the baking powder, salt, and lemon zest in a large bowl. Add the cold butter pieces and cut into the flour until crumbly. Mix in the cream until the dough is just moistened. Press together and pat into a loose ball. Cover and refrigerate for 20 minutes.

3 Preheat the oven to 425°F. To form each biscuit, gather 3 tablespoons of dough and form into a ball; each ball should be about 1 inch smaller in diameter than the jars you are using. Place the balls of dough on a parchment-paper-lined cookie sheet 2 to 3 inches apart. Brush with the melted butter and sprinkle with some granulated sugar. Bake for 9 to 10 minutes, until golden brown. Remove from the oven and allow to cool.

4 Make the whipped cream: Beat the cream and confectioners' sugar together with a handheld mixer until stiff peaks form.

5 Place a biscuit flat side up in each jar. Spoon ¼ cup of the strawberries and their liquid over each biscuit, and top with the whipped cream. Place another biscuit on top, and, if you like, garnish with mint sprigs. Serve immediately.

ginger
mascarpone *with caramelized apricots*

FOR THE FLAVORED MASCARPONE

2 cups pasteurized whipping cream (approximately 35% fat content)

1 tablespoon fresh lemon juice

1 teaspoon vanilla extract

3 tablespoons candied ginger pieces

FOR THE APRICOTS

½ cup raw honey

6 ripe apricots, halved and pitted

MAKES 6 individual desserts

There is something intensely satisfying about homemade
cheese, and mascarpone is one of the easiest places to start. It is paired with apricots kissed with honey in this creamy treat, a dessert guests will gush over.

—————— • ——————

1 In a double-boiler over simmering water, heat the cream, stirring frequently, until it reaches 190°F on a candy thermometer. Add the lemon juice, stirring constantly. Continue stirring over the heat until the cream curdles and thickens to the point that it covers the back of a wooden spoon.

2 Remove the cream from the heat and allow to cool for about 20 minutes. Place a strainer in a medium bowl and line it with 4 pieces of cheesecloth. Transfer the mascarpone to the strainer and cover it completely with the cheesecloth, being careful not to squeeze or push on the cheese. Allow the cheese to cool completely and then transfer it, in the bowl and strainer, to the refrigerator. Let the cheese drain and chill for 12 to 24 hours.

3 Remove the mascarpone from the cheesecloth, place it in a bowl, and stir in the vanilla. Stir in the ginger pieces until they are incorporated throughout. Set aside.

4 Preheat the broiler. Place the honey in a small bowl and dip the cut sides of the apricot halves in the honey to coat. Put the apricot halves honeyed side up on a baking sheet. Place the baking sheet under the broiler. Watch carefully for the honey to caramelize, 4 to 5 minutes, then remove from the oven. Spoon two apricot halves into each of six 8-ounce jars. Top each jar with 2 to 3 tablespoons of the flavored mascarpone. Serve immediately.

banana buttermilk *trifles*

FOR THE CAKE

1 cup granulated sugar

8 tablespoons (1 stick) unsalted butter, softened

¼ cup buttermilk

1 teaspoon vanilla extract

1 large egg

3 overripe bananas

2 cups all-purpose flour

2 teaspoons baking powder

½ teaspoon salt

FOR THE PUDDING

⅓ cup granulated sugar

3 tablespoons cornstarch

⅛ teaspoon salt

Vanilla bean seeds scraped from 1 vanilla bean pod

3 large egg yolks

2 cups whole milk

2 tablespoons unsalted butter, at room temperature, cut into pieces

6 ripe bananas

Bananas are capable of an amazing feat, turning in what

appears to be the blink of an eye from green-hued and firm to spotted so thickly with brown that the yellow is barely visible. No complaints, though, for it's those brown-speckled numbers that make the best dessert.

———— • ————

1 Make the cake: Preheat the oven to 350°F. Line a 9 × 13-inch baking pan with parchment paper. Cream together the sugar and butter for 2 minutes. Add the buttermilk, vanilla, and egg and mix on low speed until blended. Mash the bananas slightly, add them to the bowl, and mix well on low speed.

2 In a separate bowl, whisk together the flour, baking powder, and salt. Mix the dry ingredients into the wet ones just until incorporated. Spread the cake batter onto the baking pan in an even layer.

3 Bake the cake for 25 to 30 minutes, or until a toothpick inserted into the center comes out clean. Remove from the oven and allow to cool completely.

recipe continues

1 cup heavy cream

2 tablespoons confectioners' sugar

MAKES 10 individual trifles

4 Make the pudding: Whisk together the granulated sugar, cornstarch, salt, and vanilla bean seeds in a medium saucepan. Whisk in the egg yolks until well combined. Slowly pour in the milk, whisking to incorporate it. Cook the mixture over medium-low heat until it thickens, about 10 to 15 minutes. Remove from the heat and whisk in the butter one piece at a time, making sure each piece is incorporated before adding the next. Cover the top of the pudding with plastic wrap and refrigerate until cool, 1½ to 2 hours.

5 Using the top of an 8-ounce jar as a guide, cut 10 circles from the cake. Fit the circles into the bottoms of ten 8-ounce jars. Slice the ripe bananas ¼ inch thick and line the sides of the jars with the banana slices pressed up against the glass, two slices deep. Pour the pudding into the jars to cover the bananas.

6 In a medium bowl, beat together the heavy cream and the confectioners' sugar until stiff peaks form. Spoon the whipped cream over the pudding. Refrigerate until ready to serve.

how to pick
jars for desserts

To some extent, putting desserts into individual servings in jars should be convenient. If you are already making jams and jellies, then finding jars will be as easy as raiding your canning supplies. If, however, you're looking to purchase jars specifically for this purpose or to give as gifts, here are a few things to consider when shopping.

First, choose jars that are appropriate for their purpose. These are dessert recipes and, as such, should be made in small portions to account for their richness. Look for those cute little jars in the 4- to 8-ounce range to house your desserts. The 8-ounce jars will be the perfect size for baking cupcakes, leaving plenty of room for frosting and putting on the covers to transport easily. They're also a great size for ice cream treats and fruit crisps. The smaller sizes work well for rich desserts like pots de crème and cheesecake. One-quart jars are good for mixes, the subject of the last chapter in this book.

Next, look at the lids. If you're planning on reusing the jars for canning purposes after you use them for these desserts, the cheaper the replacement lids or rings are the better. If you'll be giving these jars away, you'll want to look at the design of the jars' lids. Whether you want to cover the lids in fabric or simply tie a string and a cute letterpress tag to the jar will make a difference in which jars to choose.

In short, choose jars that are on the small side and take into account the future use of the jar after it's been filled with a dessert. Remember that jars can be used again and again, making them great for multiple uses and, therefore, environmentally friendly.

sparkling pomegranate & orange jelly cups

1 (750ml) bottle sparkling white grape juice

2 (¼-ounce) envelopes unflavored gelatin

¾ cup water

¼ cup sugar

5 oranges

2 cups fresh pomegranate arils (seeds)

MAKES 6 to 12 individual jelly cups

These jelly cups are full of delightful bursts of juicy, red pomegranate seeds and orange slices. Made with sparkling grape juice, this is a light and fruity dessert that blows grandma's gelatin mold out of the water.

————— • —————

1 Pour the grape juice into a large bowl or measuring cup. Sprinkle the gelatin over the grape juice and set aside.

2 In a small saucepan over medium-high heat, combine the water and sugar and cook, stirring occasionally, until the sugar is dissolved. Remove from the heat and pour over the grape juice and gelatin. Stir until the gelatin is dissolved.

3 Cut the peel and pith off the oranges and discard. Slice the oranges approximately ⅜ inch thick. In six 8-ounce jars or twelve 4-ounce jars, layer the oranges and pomegranate arils until they are ½ inch from the top of each jar. Slowly pour the grape juice and gelatin mixture through a fine-mesh strainer over the fruit until all the fruit is covered.

4 Cover and refrigerate the jars for 6 hours, or until the jelly is firm. Serve cold.

frozen desserts

frozen mudslide pies

FOR THE CRUST

1 cup chocolate cookie crumbs

2 tablespoons unsalted butter, melted

FOR THE ESPRESSO GANACHE

8 ounces bittersweet chocolate, chopped

¾ cup heavy cream

¾ teaspoon instant espresso powder

1 teaspoon vanilla extract

FOR THE CHOCOLATE FILLING

1 cup heavy cream

¾ cup confectioners' sugar

3 tablespoons cocoa powder

FOR THE WHIPPED CREAM

½ cup heavy cream

1 tablespoon confectioners' sugar

Espresso powder, for garnish

MAKES 8 individual mudslide pies

A mudslide of coffee and chocolate is one I don't mind

jumping into headfirst. Chocolate cookies and smooth chocolate offset the bite the espresso ganache brings, all topped with a cloud of sweet, soft whipped cream.

•

1 Make the crust: Mix the cookie crumbs and butter until the crumbs are evenly coated. Press 2 tablespoons of the crumbs into the bottom of each of eight 8-ounce jars and set aside.

2 Make the ganache: Place the chocolate in a heatproof bowl. In a small, heavy-bottomed saucepan, heat the heavy cream over medium heat just until it boils. Remove from the heat and pour over the chocolate pieces. Allow to stand for 1 minute and then whisk in the espresso powder and vanilla until all the chocolate is melted and the mixture is smooth. Pour evenly into the jars over the chocolate crust. Refrigerate the jars until the ganache is firm, about 30 minutes.

3 Make the chocolate filling: Beat together the heavy cream, confectioners' sugar, and cocoa in a medium-size bowl until stiff peaks form. Using a pastry bag and tip, preferably, or a zip-top bag with a corner cut off, pipe the filling over the espresso ganache layer. Cover loosely and freeze for at least 2 hours, until ready to serve.

4 Make the whipped cream: Beat together the heavy cream and confectioners' sugar. Pipe a small dollop onto the top of each pie and sprinkle with espresso powder. Serve immediately.

ice cream cakes
in a jar

FOR THE BROWNIE CRUST

¾ cup granulated sugar

6 tablespoons (¾ stick) unsalted butter, melted

1 tablespoon water

1 large egg

1 teaspoon vanilla extract

¾ cup all-purpose flour

½ cup unsweetened cocoa powder

¼ teaspoon baking powder

Pinch of salt

FOR THE ICE CREAM CAKE

5 cups chocolate ice cream, slightly softened

2½ cups vanilla ice cream, slightly softened

1 cup chocolate cookie crumbs

½ recipe Chocolate Sauce, page 123

4 ounces milk chocolate, broken up

¼ cup mini chocolate chips, for garnish

MAKES 10 individual ice cream cakes

Creamy vanilla and chocolate ice cream are layered together with a brownie crust, with plenty of chocolate fudge holding it all together. An ice cream cake is the quintessential summer birthday delight. Guests can simply snap up their cup from the ice bucket and be on their way, spoon in one hand, creamy, cool dessert in the other.

———————— • ————————

1 Make the brownie crust: Preheat the oven to 350°F and lightly grease an 8-inch square pan. Mix together the sugar, butter, and water in a medium-size bowl. Stir in the egg and vanilla. In a separate bowl, sift together the flour, cocoa powder, baking powder, and salt. Add the flour mixture to the sugar mixture and stir until just combined.

2 Spread the batter into the prepared pan. Bake for 15 to 18 minutes, until a toothpick inserted in the center comes out clean. Remove from the oven and allow to cool completely.

3 Crumble the cooled brownie. Scoop a generous 3 tablespoons of brownie crumbs into the bottoms of each of ten 8-ounce jars and press down. Press about ½ cup chocolate ice cream into each jar, using a spoon to level the layer. Add 1½ tablespoons of cookie crumbs and then drizzle 2 tablespoons of chocolate sauce over them. Add ¼ cup vanilla ice cream to each jar and press down. Transfer the jars to the freezer until the ice cream is again firm.

4 In a double boiler over simmering water, melt the milk chocolate and place in a small piping bag. Snip the tip or use a small piping tip to decorate the tops of the vanilla ice cream with the melted chocolate. Garnish with the mini chocolate chips. Place the jars back in the freezer until ready to eat.

"fried" ice cream

2 cups cornflakes, crushed

¼ cup granulated sugar

1 teaspoon ground cinnamon

4 tablespoons (½ stick) unsalted butter, melted

½ gallon cinnamon- or vanilla-flavored ice cream, slightly softened

FOR THE HONEY CARAMEL SAUCE

1 cup honey

1 cup evaporated milk

8 tablespoons (1 stick) unsalted butter

1 teaspoon vanilla extract

Pinch of salt

MAKES 10 individual ice cream desserts

To create that fried ice cream flavor you know so well

without the deep-fat frying, this creamy confection boasts cornflake crunch and plenty of honey. These jars can be made ahead and stored in the freezer until ready to serve.

———————— • ————————

1 Stir together the cornflakes, sugar, and cinnamon in a bowl. Drizzle the butter over the top and toss until well coated. Press 2 generous tablespoons of the cornflake crumble in the bottoms of each of ten 8-ounce jars. Set aside the remaining crumble. Pack the ice cream into the jars to just below the lip, and then freeze the jars until the ice cream is firm.

2 Make the honey caramel sauce: Combine the honey, evaporated milk, and butter in a medium-size saucepan and bring just to a boil over medium-high heat, stirring constantly. Reduce the heat to medium and continue to cook, stirring frequently, for 10 to 12 minutes, until the caramel sauce is thick and dark brown. Remove from the heat and stir in the vanilla and salt. Allow to cool slightly.

3 When ready to serve, remove the jars from the freezer and top with the remaining cornflake crumble. Drizzle the honey caramel sauce over the top and serve.

cinnamon-spiced affogatos

Ground espresso beans, enough for 4 shots

1 teaspoon ground cinnamon, plus more for garnish

¼ teaspoon ground allspice

2 cups caramel or salted caramel gelato

MAKES 4 individual affogatos

A twist on the classic affogato, which consists of vanilla gelato

and espresso, this one uses a caramel gelato in place of the vanilla and spices up the espresso with a bit of cinnamon and allspice. It's a spicy take on the coffee float.

•

1 Stir together the ground espresso beans with the cinnamon and allspice. Brew the spiced espresso according to the manufacturer's directions.

2 Add ½ cup gelato to the bottoms of four 8-ounce jars. Pour the hot espresso over the gelato. Sprinkle with a bit of additional cinnamon and serve immediately.

frozen banana splits

1 cup graham cracker crumbs

2 tablespoons granulated sugar

2 tablespoons unsalted butter, melted

5 bananas, peeled, cut in chunks, and frozen

1 (8-ounce) can crushed pineapple in 100% juice, drained

1 cup fresh strawberries, hulled and sliced

¼ cup chocolate sauce; recipe follows

1 cup heavy cream

2 tablespoons confectioners' sugar

8 maraschino cherries

MAKES 8 individual banana splits

Here is a fun spin on the traditional banana split.

Rather than using ice cream as the glue that holds all the sweet treats together, these banana splits rely instead on frozen banana. With a bit of pineapple and chocolate, a touch of strawberry, and a swirl of whipped cream, this cherry-topped treat would be a welcome surprise at your backyard celebration.

⎯⎯⎯⎯⎯ • ⎯⎯⎯⎯⎯

1 Mix together the graham cracker crumbs, granulated sugar, and butter in a bowl. Divide the graham cracker mixture evenly among eight 8-ounce jars, and press the mixture into the bottoms of the jars.

2 In a food processor, blend the frozen banana chunks until smooth. Scoop on top of the graham cracker mixture and level off. Add one ounce of crushed pineapple to the top of each jar and follow with the strawberries. Drizzle chocolate sauce over the strawberries. (Reserve any leftover chocolate sauce for another use.)

3 Beat the cream and the confectioners' sugar in a medium-size bowl until stiff peaks form. Pipe or spoon the whipped cream over the chocolate sauce and top each jar with a maraschino cherry. Serve immediately.

chocolate sauce

½ cup heavy cream

2 tablespoons water

2 tablespoons unsweetened cocoa powder

2 tablespoons granulated sugar

2 tablespoons light corn syrup

Pinch of salt

7 ounces bittersweet chocolate, chopped

1 tablespoon unsalted butter

1 teaspoon vanilla extract

In a small saucepan, heat the cream, water, cocoa powder, sugar, corn syrup, and salt over medium heat, stirring frequently, until the mixture just begins to boil. Remove from the heat and stir in the chocolate, butter, and vanilla until smooth. Allow to cool slightly. The sauce can be made ahead and stored in the refrigerator; reheat it slightly before pouring over your dessert.

MAKES about 1 cup chocolate sauce

basil strawberry–
lemonade granitas

1 cup sugar

1 handful fresh basil leaves

1 cup water

4 cups fresh strawberries, hulled and sliced

Juice and finely grated zest of 2 lemons

Lemon slices, for garnish

MAKES 10 individual granitas

All the freshness of a warm summer's evening is combined

into a refreshing jar of delight. The aromatic basil adds a light accent to this classic summer treat, which is blended together and frozen right in the jar for a grab-and-go dessert that's ready to help you tackle—or unwind from—a hot summer day.

————— • —————

1 Combine the sugar and basil leaves with the water in a medium-size saucepan. Heat over medium heat, stirring occasionally, until the sugar is completely dissolved. Remove from the heat and let cool. When the simple syrup mixture is cool, remove and discard the basil leaves.

2 Combine the strawberries, lemon juice, and lemon zest in a blender or food processor. Pulse until smooth. Pour the cooled simple syrup into the strawberry mixture and blend well.

3 Fill ten 8-ounce jars three-quarters full with the strawberry mixture. Cover loosely and place in the freezer for 30 minutes. Scrape down the edges of the jars with a fork and stir the scrapings into the centers. Return the jars to the freezer for 90 minutes, and scrape them down again. Freeze for an additional 3 hours until frozen through.

4 When you are ready to serve the granita, use a fork to stir the granita mixture one more time. Serve ice cold, garnished with lemon slices.

peach granita bellinis

½ cup sugar

½ cup water

3 medium-size peaches, peeled and cut into wedges

1 tablespoon fresh lemon juice

1 (750ml) bottle Prosecco or sparkling white grape juice

MAKES 8 dessert drinks

A Venetian cocktail in frozen form becomes a refreshing

dessert. If you're a Bellini aficionado, you'll want to make a batch of these and store them in the freezer for an aperitif on the patio before dinner.

———— • ————

1 Combine the sugar and water in a small saucepan over medium heat and cook, stirring frequently, until all the sugar is dissolved. Remove the simple syrup from the heat and cool slightly.

2 Combine the peaches, lemon juice, and simple syrup in a blender and pulse until smooth. Spoon approximately ¼ cup of puree into each of 8 tall pint jars. Cover, freeze for 2 hours, and stir each glass with a fork. Continue to freeze for an additional 3 hours.

3 Remove the jars from the freezer and uncover. Use a fork to loosen the granita mixture one more time. Top off each jar with the Prosecco and serve immediately.

mixes for giving

cranberry-walnut
quick bread mix 130

cinnamon coffee cake mix 133

espresso brownies mix 134

monster cookies mix 137

white chocolate spice
cookies mix 138

spiced hot chocolate mix with
cinnamon marshmallows 140

campfire bars mix 145

cranberry-walnut
quick bread mix

1¾ cups all-purpose flour

2½ teaspoons baking powder

½ teaspoon salt

1 cup walnuts, chopped

1 cup dried cranberries

½ cup packed light brown sugar

¾ cup granulated sugar

Vanilla bean seeds scraped from 1 vanilla bean pod

MAKES 1 jar of quick bread mix, to yield one loaf of bread

Quick breads have split personalities. They can play

the part of the dessert, sweet and comforting after a savory meal, but they can also do an about-face and become a breakfast item, warm and slathered with butter. However you choose to eat your quick bread, this one makes a delightful choice for a gift.

———————— • ————————

1 Mix together the flour, baking powder, and salt in a bowl. Place in a 1-quart jar. Layer the walnuts on top, followed by the cranberries and then the brown sugar, packing down the brown sugar lightly to hold it in place.

2 Mix together the sugar and vanilla bean seeds and add to the jar as the top layer. Seal with the lid, decorate the jar if you like, and attach a label with these instructions for the recipient:

TO MAKE CRANBERRY-WALNUT QUICK BREAD

2 LARGE EGGS • ³/4 CUP WHOLE MILK

4 TABLESPOONS (¹/2 STICK) UNSALTED BUTTER, MELTED

Preheat the oven to 350°F. Grease a loaf pan. Beat together the eggs, milk, and butter in a bowl. Add all the contents of the jar and mix until just combined. Pour into the loaf pan and bake for 45 to 50 minutes, until the top is golden brown and a toothpick inserted in the center comes out clean. Flip pan on its side and let the bread cool slightly before removing from the pan and cooling on a wire rack.

cinnamon
coffee cake mix

2 cups all-purpose flour

1 teaspoon baking soda

1 teaspoon baking powder

1½ teaspoons ground cinnamon

½ cup cinnamon chips

1 cup sugar

Vanilla bean seeds scraped from 1 vanilla bean pod

½ cup chopped pecans

MAKES 1 jar of cake mix, to yield one 9-inch-square cake

A good cinnamon coffee cake is not to be messed with. It's the

perfect accompaniment to that first cup of java in the morning, and your friends will be grateful when you make its preparation as easy as mixing it and popping it in the oven.

———————— • ————————

1 Mix together the flour, baking soda, baking powder, and ground cinnamon in a bowl. Place in a 1-quart jar. Top with a layer of cinnamon chips.

2 Mix together the sugar and the vanilla bean seeds and add as a layer in the jar. Top with the chopped pecans. Seal with the lid, decorate the jar if you like, and attach a label with these instructions for the recipient:

TO MAKE CINNAMON COFFEE CAKE

8 TABLESPOONS (1 STICK) UNSALTED BUTTER, SOFTENED

2 LARGE EGGS

1 CUP SOUR CREAM OR GREEK-STYLE YOGURT

1/4 CUP WHOLE MILK

Preheat the oven to 350°F. Grease and flour a 9-inch square baking pan. Mix together the butter, eggs, and yogurt in a large bowl until well blended. Stir in all the contents of the jar, then slowly stir in the milk. Pour into the prepared pan and bake for 30 to 35 minutes, until a toothpick inserted into the center comes out clean. Remove from the oven and let cool slightly. Serve warm.

espresso
brownies mix

1¼ cups all-purpose flour

½ teaspoon baking powder

¼ teaspoon salt

¾ cup unsweetened Dutch-process cocoa powder

2 teaspoons espresso powder

½ cup chopped walnuts

1½ cups sugar

6 ounces dark chocolate, coarsely chopped

MAKES 1 jar of brownie mix, to yield 24 brownies

Chocolate and espresso come together in a thoughtful and

elegant gift for the chocolate lover in your family. These brownies bake up moist and chewy for a divine treat.

———————— • ————————

1 Sift together the flour, baking powder, and salt, and pour the mixture into a 1-quart jar. Stir together the cocoa and espresso powder and add to the jar on top of the flour mixture.

2 Layer the walnuts on top, followed by a layer of sugar and a layer of dark chocolate. Seal with the lid, decorate the jar if you like, and attach a label with these instructions for the recipient:

TO MAKE ESPRESSO BROWNIES

12 TABLESPOONS (1½ STICKS) UNSALTED BUTTER, MELTED . . . .

2 LARGE EGGS • 2 TEASPOONS VANILLA EXTRACT . . . .

Preheat the oven to 350°F and lightly grease a 9 x 13-inch baking pan. Pour the contents of the jar into a large bowl and whisk them together. Add the butter, eggs, and vanilla. Stir well. Spread the batter into the prepared pan and bake for 20 to 25 minutes, until a toothpick inserted into the center comes out clean. Let cool completely, cut into squares, and serve.

monster cookies mix

½ cup granulated sugar

1 teaspoon baking soda

½ teaspoon salt

2¼ cups rolled oats

¾ cup candy-coated chocolate candies or chocolate chips

½ cup packed light brown sugar

¼ cup chopped walnuts

MAKES 1 jar of cookie mix, to yield 24 large cookies

The classic kitchen-sink cookie, these are easy to customize to

the recipient's individual tastes simply by switching out candies and nuts. They are soft and chewy with a crisp outer layer, and you'll surely get requests to share the mix recipe after all the cookies have been consumed. These make fabulous welcome gifts, which is how they were first shared with me.

————— • —————

1 Mix together the granulated sugar, baking soda, and salt in a bowl. Pour into a 1-quart Mason jar.

2 Top with a layer of half of the oats. Add the candies in a layer, and top with a layer of brown sugar. Top with a layer of the remaining oats and then a layer of walnuts. Seal with the lid, decorate the jar if you like, and attach a label with these instructions for the recipient:

TO MAKE MONSTER COOKIES

3/4 CUP SMOOTH OR CHUNKY PEANUT BUTTER (NOT NATURAL)

2 TABLESPOONS UNSALTED BUTTER, SOFTENED

1 TEASPOON VANILLA EXTRACT • 2 EGGS, LIGHTLY BEATEN

Preheat the oven to 350°F. Mix together the peanut butter, butter, vanilla, and eggs in a bowl. Add the contents of this jar. Form the dough into 2-inch balls and set on cookie sheets 2 inches apart. Bake for 12 to 14 minutes, until the tops of the cookies begin to brown. Allow to cool completely on a wire rack.

white chocolate
spice cookies mix

2½ cups all-purpose flour

1 teaspoon baking soda

¼ teaspoon salt

⅓ cup packed light brown sugar

1 cup granulated sugar

1½ teaspoons ground ginger

½ teaspoon ground cinnamon

¼ teaspoon ground cardamom

Vanilla bean seeds scraped from 1 vanilla bean pod

1 cup white chocolate chunks or chips

MAKES 1 jar of cookie mix, to yield 18 to 24 cookies

Some people go weak in the knees for crunchy gingersnaps,
while others prefer the chewy consistency of a molasses cookie. These spice cookies meet you somewhere in the middle. They have a gingersnap flavor with a slight crunch on the outside and plenty of chew in the center. Sugar and spice and everything nice, all wrapped into a cute little jar just begging to be given to the cookie lover on your list.

———————— • ————————

1 Whisk together the flour, baking soda, and salt in a bowl. Place in a 1-quart jar. Top with a layer of brown sugar.

2 In a separate bowl, mix together the granulated sugar, ginger, cinnamon, cardamom, and vanilla bean seeds until the ingredients are well combined and the spices are evenly distributed in the sugar. Add this sugar mixture to the jar and top with the white chocolate chunks or chips. Seal with the lid, decorate the jar if you like, and attach a label with the following instructions for the recipient:

note: Adding vanilla bean seeds to the mix means fewer ingredients for recipients to add when they want to make the cookies. What to do with all those leftover vanilla bean hulls? Clean and dry the pods completely first. Now, you can submerge the pods in sugar to create vanilla sugar, or add them to syrups and hot drinks to impart some vanilla flavor. Or you can grind dried used pods and add to sugar, ice cream, or cookies for a bit of vanilla essence.

TO MAKE WHITE CHOCOLATE SPICE COOKIES

8 TABLESPOONS (1 STICK) UNSALTED BUTTER, SOFTENED

1/4 CUP FULL-FLAVOR MOLASSES

1 LARGE EGG · 1/2 CUP GRANULATED SUGAR

Preheat the oven to 325°F. Place the butter and molasses in the bowl of a stand mixer and mix until smooth. Beat in the egg. Add all the contents of the jar and mix until incorporated. Roll into balls 1 inch in diameter, roll the balls in the sugar, and place them on a parchment-lined baking sheet 2 inches apart. Bake for 8 to 10 minutes, until the tops are cracked and the edges have started to brown. Cool slightly on the baking sheet before transferring to a wire rack to cool completely. Store in an airtight container.

spiced
hot chocolate mix
with cinnamon marshmallows

FOR THE MARSHMALLOWS

¾ cup cold water

3 (¼-ounce) envelopes unflavored gelatin

2 cups granulated sugar

½ cup light corn syrup

½ teaspoon ground cinnamon

¼ teaspoon salt

2 teaspoons powdered egg white, with enough water to reconstitute according to the manufacturer's directions

2 teaspoons vanilla extract

Confectioners' sugar, for dusting

Cinnamon and a touch of cayenne give this hot chocolate

a bit of a kick, while soft and fluffy homemade marshmallows sweeten the deal and make a complete gift or stocking stuffer for the holiday season.

———— • ————

1 Make the marshmallows: Into the bowl of a stand mixer fitted with the whisk attachment or in a large heatproof bowl, pour ½ cup of the cold water and sprinkle the gelatin over the top. Let stand for 10 minutes to soften.

2 In a heavy-bottomed saucepan, combine the granulated sugar and corn syrup with the remaining ¼ cup cold water. Add the cinnamon and salt and stir over medium heat until the sugar is dissolved. Increase the heat and bring to a boil. Boil hard for 1 minute.

3 Pour the boiling syrup into the gelatin and beat at high speed in the stand mixer, or using a handheld mixer, for 10 to 12 minutes, until the mixture is thick and white and has tripled in size.

4 In a clean bowl, mix together the powdered egg white and the water to reconstitute. Beat with a handheld mixer until stiff peaks form. Add the egg white and the vanilla to the gelatin mixture and beat just until mixed thoroughly.

recipe continues

4 cups confectioners' sugar

2 cups unsweetened Dutch-process cocoa powder

4 teaspoons cornstarch

2 teaspoons ground cinnamon

½ teaspoon salt

1 pinch cayenne pepper, or more to taste

MAKES 5 jars of hot chocolate mix with marshmallows

5 Dust a 10 × 15-inch jellyroll pan with confectioners' sugar. Pour the marshmallow mixture into the pan and spread evenly. Dust with ¼ cup confectioners' sugar and place, uncovered, in the refrigerator for 3 hours, or until firm.

6 Loosen the marshmallow mixture from the edges of the pan and turn out onto a cutting board. Slice into 1-inch squares. Set aside.

7 Prepare the hot chocolate mix: Sift together all of the hot chocolate mix ingredients. Using a wide funnel or spoon, pour 1½ cups hot chocolate mix into each of five 8-ounce jars. Top with cut marshmallows to fill the jar. (You will have extra marshmallows; reserve them for another use.) Screw the lids in place and top with a circle of fabric and a raffia tie. Include the following directions on a tag or label on the jar:

TO MAKE HOT CHOCOLATE

Spoon ¼ cup of mix into a mug. Heat 1 cup of milk until hot but not boiling. Pour the milk over the cocoa mix while stirring or whisking. Top with marshmallows.

jar portability

I was headed to a friend's house with my family. While the children splashed nearby, the cooking would happen outside. These are some of my favorite moments in the summer, slow and relaxed, with all the time in the world to cook and eat.

For my part, I was bringing dessert, something easy and elegant that fit the rest of the meal but did not overpower in its sweetness. Immediately *pots de crème* (page 77) came to mind. When it came time to fill glasses or ramekins, I reached instead for the Mason jars I had on the shelf. Topped with lids and ready to go, they were easy simply to add to a basket, and we were on our way.

The beauty of using Mason jars to store cakes and desserts is that the desserts instantly become more portable than they otherwise would be. Lids and sturdy sides make tossing a cake into the picnic basket an exceptionally easy task rather than one that requires careful handling to prevent tilting and teetering.

Add filled jars to coolers filled with ice or to towel-lined baskets for carrying to picnics, backyard barbecues, and dinner parties. Larger numbers can be packed tightly and layered in boxes for the car ride to the venue. Cakes that have a bit of a longer shelf life can be hugged with bubble wrap, tucked into boxes, and shipped to loved ones far from home.

campfire bars *mix*

1 cup graham cracker pieces, each about 1-inch square

1½ cups mini marsh-mallows, homemade (recipe, page 140) or store-bought

¾ cup milk chocolate chips

½ cup granola

⅓ cup packed light brown sugar

½ cup chopped almonds

MAKES 1 jar of campfire bars mix, to yield about 16 bars

The smell of wood burning, marshmallows roasting to a

golden brown, sticky fingers, and mouths full of happiness: Everyone loves a toasty s'more. The melted chocolate and gooey marshmallow surrounded by crunchy crackers give you the taste of a hearty trail mix as you enjoy a walk through the woods. Here all the flavors of camping are tucked inside a quick and easy mix for giving.

———— • ————

In a 1-quart jar, layer the graham crackers, marshmallows, chocolate chips, granola, brown sugar, and almonds. Seal with the lid, decorate the jar if you like, and attach a label with these instructions for the recipient:

TO MAKE CAMPFIRE BARS

8 TABLESPOONS (1 STICK) UNSALTED BUTTER, MELTED ....

Preheat the oven to 350°F. Pour all the contents of the jar into a large bowl. Stir in the melted butter until all the pieces are coated. Press into a 9-inch square baking pan. Bake for 12 to 15 minutes. Allow to cool. Cut into bars and serve.

acknowledgments

I grew up fascinated by the kitchen and the ability it gave me to create a kind of artwork

that would nourish others. Cracking open my first cookbook before the age of five and making a full dinner for my family by the age of seven, I was smitten by the smells and sounds and the ultimate reward: feeding the ones you love.

———————— • ————————

The process that brought me to actually writing my own cookbook was a long and varied path, and without the help of so many others it would have never become a reality.

Thank you to my agent, Meg Thompson, who continually pushes me to create, and to The Harvard Common Press, who believed in this project from the beginning. A special thanks goes out to Dan Rosenberg for calling me on a hot summer day to propose that I write this book and then for holding my hand through the entire process from the early stages to the final edits. His attention to detail, support, and words of wisdom were essential to the book. Thanks to the wonderful team—Virginia Downes, Pat Jalbert-Levine, Nancy Grant Mahoney, Adam Salomone, and Bruce Shaw, along with freelance editors Andrea Chesman and Jane Dornbusch—and everyone else at HCP who approached the book with enthusiasm and a creative eye.

To my dear friends and readers in the online space, I could never accurately tell you how much your kind words of encouragement and support have meant to me over the months I spent working on this cookbook. Thank you to Amanda who opened her house to me, Mandi for being my biggest fan and target audience, and to everyone else who helped and was there for me, including but not limited to Aimee, Amanda, Amber, Amy, Brooke, Cheryl, Danielle, Jamie, Jen, Jessica, Julie, Kathy, Katie, Kristen, Maria, Michelle, Paula, Shari, the two Stephs, Sylvie, Tara, Tracy, Zoë, and so many more. Thanks to my neighbors, Mike, Sara, Shawn, Kali, Doug, and Sarah, for taste-testing and then tasting again; to my mom for letting me make yeast bread at the age of seven, and to my sisters, brothers, and dad for eating my meals; and to my friends for understanding when I couldn't come out to play.

Special thanks to my four children for helping to fill jars, holding props for the photos, and waiting patiently when dinner was late. A depth of gratitude to my husband for allowing me the time and space to create and for continuously picking me up off the floor to encourage me to keep going. Without you, there is very little to me. And to Jesus, of course.

measurement equivalents

Please note that all conversions are approximate.

LIQUID CONVERSIONS

U.S.	IMPERIAL	METRIC
1 tsp	—	5 ml
1 tbs	½ fl oz	15 ml
2 tbs	1 fl oz	30 ml
3 tbs	1 ½ fl oz	45 ml
¼ cup	2 fl oz	60 ml
⅓ cup	2 ½ fl oz	75 ml
⅓ cup + 1 tbs	3 fl oz	90 ml
⅓ cup + 2 tbs	3 ½ fl oz	100 ml
½ cup	4 fl oz	120 ml
⅔ cup	5 fl oz	150 ml
¾ cup	6 fl oz	180 ml
¾ cup + 2 tbs	7 fl oz	200 ml
1 cup	8 fl oz	240 ml
1 cup + 2 tbs	9 fl oz	275 ml
1 ¼ cups	10 fl oz	300 ml
1 ⅓ cups	11 fl oz	325 ml
1 ½ cups	12 fl oz	350 ml
1 ⅔ cups	13 fl oz	375 ml
1 ¾ cups	14 fl oz	400 ml
1 ¾ cups + 2 tbs	15 fl oz	450 ml
2 cups (1 pint)	16 fl oz	475 ml
2 ½ cups	20 fl oz	600 ml
3 cups	24 fl oz	720 ml
4 cups (1 quart)	32 fl oz	945 ml
		(1,000 ml is 1 liter)

WEIGHT CONVERSIONS

U.S./U.K.	METRIC
½ oz	14 g
1 oz	28 g
1½ oz	43 g
2 oz	57 g
2½ oz	71 g
3 oz	85 g
3½ oz	100 g
4 oz	113 g
5 oz	142 g
6 oz	170 g
7 oz	200 g
8 oz	227 g
9 oz	255 g
10 oz	284 g
11 oz	312 g
12 oz	340 g
13 oz	368 g
14 oz	400 g
15 oz	425 g
1 lb	454 g

OVEN TEMPERATURE CONVERSIONS

°F	GAS MARK	°C
250	½	120
275	1	140
300	2	150
325	3	165
350	4	180
375	5	190
400	6	200
425	7	220
450	8	230
475	9	240
500	10	260
550	Broil	290

index

about
the author

Shaina Olmanson is the creator of the widely read blog Food for My Family, which can be found at www.foodformyfamily.com. She creates the food, writes the recipes and other copy, and shoots the photographs for the blog. The blog was ranked in the top ten in Babble.com's 2011 list of the 100 best food blogs for moms, and it also was named a "Top 10 Family Cooking Blog" by My Life Scoop. Shaina is a regular contributor to the blogs Simple Bites and Life Your Way as well as to Babble's Family Kitchen, and she has served as the editor of the food channel for Lifetime Moms, a digital property of the A&E Networks. She lives in the Minneapolis–St. Paul area with her husband, Ole, and their four children.